Sell Your House with No Agent and No Commission

The For Sale by Owner Revolution

Keywords

Real estate

Redfin

Zillow

Home selling

Realty

Brokerage

Home value

For sale by owner: Show me the money!

So you're thinking about selling your house without a real estate agent, huh? Well, you're definitely not alone. More and more homeowners are choosing the For Sale by Owner (FSBO for short) these days, and there are a ton of reasons why.

First of all, let's talk about the elephant in the room: saving money. I mean, who doesn't love saving a big wad of cash? When you sell your house with a real estate agent, you typically have to fork over a commission fee, which can range anywhere from 5 to 6 percent of the sale price. That's a big chunk of change, especially if you're selling a high-priced home. But when you sell your house without an agent, you get to keep that money for yourself—tens of thousands of dollars, depending on the price range of your home. I mean, just think about all the things you could do with an extra share of the sale. That's like a whole new kitchen, or a fancy vacation, or... well, you get the idea.

Exactly how much money are we talking about? Let's do some math, shall we? Let's say you're a "For Sale by Owner," or FSBO for short. Your home is worth a cool $350,000. The average commission for a real estate agent is around 6%. So, if you were to use an agent, you'd be looking at paying them a commission of $21,000.

But, if you decide to go the FSBO route, you get to keep all of that commission money for yourself! That's like winning the lottery, except you don't have to share it with anyone else.

If you're looking to save some money and enjoy the satisfaction of selling your home on your own terms, consider going the FSBO route. Who needs agents anyway? They're like the middlemen of the real estate world and we all know middlemen are overrated. You can do this!"

In the past 10 years, the real estate business has changed dramatically. Technology has made it easier to be a FSBO—with the Internet at our fingertips, we have access to more information than ever before. Websites like Zillow and Redfin are like our own personal real estate agents, except we don't have to split the commission with them. And let's not forget about social media. Platforms like Facebook and Instagram, it's easier than ever to show off your home's best assets and find that perfect buyer. So, you can now sell your home and make a killing, all while sitting in your pajamas! It's a win-win situation.

But it's not just about the technology, it's also about empowerment. I mean, let's face it, selling your house can be a pretty daunting process. But with the right tools and information, you can do it just as well as an agent can. Plus, when you sell your house without an agent, you have more control over the process. You get to decide when to show your home, how to market it, and how to negotiate with potential buyers. There's something pretty satisfying about being in the driver's seat of such a big decision.

"Selling your home without a real estate agent is like being your own boss," said Frank. "For starters, you get to save big bucks on commission fees, which can add up to thousands of dollars. This means you get to keep more of the profit from the sale of your home and put it towards your next venture or maybe a well-deserved vacation.

"You have the power to decide how you want to market your home. Whether it's through social media, flyers, open houses or a combination of all three, you can get creative and reach out to potential buyers in the way that you see fit. You get to decide when you want to show your home, whether it's in the morning, afternoon, or evening, and you can make sure that you are available during the showings, answering any questions that potential buyers may have.

"You also get to negotiate directly with potential buyers, which can be a huge advantage. You don't have to rely on an agent to relay messages back and forth, you can get down to business and close the deal like a pro, and you can make sure that you are getting the best deal for your home.

"Selling your home without an agent does require a bit more work on your part, but the rewards are worth it. You will have more control over the sale process, and you can make sure that you are getting the best deal for your home. You will also have the opportunity to learn more about the real estate market and the process of selling a home, which

*can be useful in case you decide to sell another property in
the future.*

*"Of course, it's not always easy, and it might require
more time and effort than you originally thought, but the
sense of accomplishment that comes with selling your home
by yourself is something that can't be bought, and the
money you save on commission fees can be used to make
your next home even better.*

Now, I know what you might be thinking: "But what
about all the paperwork? And the legal stuff? That sounds
like a nightmare." And yeah, I won't sugarcoat it, there is
extra work involved when you sell your house without an
agent. But it's not as bad as you think, I promise. It's like
preparing for a final exam, you might have to study a bit
more but it's not impossible. There are a ton of resources out
there to help you navigate the legal and financial aspects of
selling a house. And honestly, it's not much different from
buying a house. You still have to fill out a bunch of forms
and make sure everything is in order, but it's not rocket
science. It's more like a jigsaw puzzle, it might be a bit
confusing but once you put it together, it all makes sense!

Information is POWER

Okay, so you're thinking about selling your house without a real estate agent, and you're wondering how things have changed when it comes to access to real estate information.

Back in the day, real estate agents had a monopoly on access to real estate information. They were the gatekeepers of information about the housing market, and if you wanted to know anything about how much your house was worth or what other houses in your area were selling for, you had to go through them. They had a big book showing all the houses for sale in their region. And believe it or not, it was against the rules for an agent to loan out that book, even to their own customer!

Now those big books are as outdated and rare as a Ford Model T. Everyone has free, instant online access to just about every scintilla of real estate information there is. Websites like Zillow and Redfin are like having a crystal ball, they give you a glimpse into the future of how much your house is worth. Within minutes, you can gauge what other houses in your area are selling for, so you can price your home competitively. It's like having a secret weapon, you'll be able to outsmart the competition and sell your home for top dollar!

And it's not just about getting information about other houses, it's also about getting information about *your* home out there. Platforms like Facebook, Instagram, and even

TikTok can help you market your home to potential buyers and get the word out about your listing.

"By selling your home yourself, you have complete control over the process, from pricing to marketing to negotiations. This can be a significant advantage, as you are able to make decisions that are in your best interest," says Gary Keller, the co-founder of Keller Williams, the biggest network of traditional real estate agents in the world.

When it's smart, and when it's dumb

Selling a house without a realtor can be a good idea in certain situations, but it's not always the best choice. Here are some examples of when it might make sense to sell your house without a realtor:

If you have experience in the real estate market and are familiar with the selling process, you may be able to handle the sale of your house on your own. This includes understanding how to price your house competitively, how to market your property effectively, and how to negotiate with potential buyers. It's like being a chef, you know how to cook up a storm and sell that house like it's a 5-star meal.

- If you are selling a house that is in a unique or niche market, such as a fixer-upper or a luxury property, you may be able to find a buyer easily without the help of a realtor. These types of properties may attract a specific type of buyer who is willing to purchase without the help of a realtor. It's like selling a rare vintage wine, it's not for everyone but the right buyer will pay a premium for it.

- This is a job. If you're willing to put in the time and effort to market your house and handle the negotiations, you may be able to save money by not hiring a realtor. This can be a good option for people who are comfortable with the selling process and have the time to devote to it. It's like a DIY project, if you're willing to put in the work, you can save money and feel a sense of accomplishment when it's done.

However, there are situations where it may *not* be a good idea to sell your house without a realtor. These include:

- If you're not familiar with the real estate market or the selling process, it can be challenging to navigate the complexities of the sale on your own. A realtor can help you with pricing your house, marketing your property, and handling negotiations with potential buyers.

- If you have a busy schedule and do not have the time to devote to the sale of your house, it may be better to hire a realtor to handle the process for you. This can be a good option for people who have demanding jobs or other time-consuming responsibilities. It's like having a personal assistant, agents take care of the nitty-gritty details so you can focus on other things.

- If your house is in a competitive market and you want to get the best price for it, a realtor may be able to help you navigate the market and negotiate the best deal for you. They have the knowledge and experience to know what buyers are looking for and how to negotiate for the best price. A realtor can help you outsmart the competition and sell your home for top dollar.
- If you aren't familiar with the legal aspects and paperwork of selling a house, a realtor can help you with that, to avoid mistakes and delays in the process. They can help you with the contract, the title search, and the closing process, ensuring that everything is done correctly and on time. It's like having a lawyer, they'll make sure everything is legal and above board.

Another question for sellers to ponder is whether they're too emotionally attached to the transaction to be an effective negotiator. It's like trying to sell your favorite toy, you might love it, but it doesn't mean someone else will. Selling a home is often an emotional process, and it can be difficult for a homeowner to detach themselves emotionally from the process and make logical, objective decisions.

One of the key advantages of working with a real estate agent is that they are trained to handle negotiations and can provide a level of detachment and objectivity that can be difficult for a homeowner to achieve.

To do it yourself, you've got to research and understand the local real estate market, as well as the market conditions specific to their property. You must also have a clear understanding of their bottom line and be prepared to walk away from a deal if the terms are not favorable. Just like with poker, you have to know when to hold 'em and when to fold 'em.

And negotiation is not just about getting the highest price possible, but also about finding a solution that is mutually beneficial for both parties. A home seller who is able to approach the negotiation process with this mindset and with a clear understanding of their goals can be successful in negotiations with a buyer. It's like haggling at a flea market, you want to walk away with a fair deal and a happy face.

Another important aspect to consider is that as a home seller, you have a better understanding of your property and you can use this knowledge to your advantage during negotiations. You know the property's strengths, weaknesses, and unique features, you can use this information to showcase the property's value to the buyer and negotiate accordingly. And you can also provide the buyer with a detailed history of the property, which can help build trust and credibility.

Not everyone has the personality to sell a home on their own. Being able to clearly and effectively communicate with the buyer, understand their needs and concerns, an earn their trust is crucial in reaching a mutually beneficial agreement. It's like being a diplomat, you have to find a common ground and make everyone happy.

"Selling a home yourself definitely has its challenges," said Stanley, who sold his first home with an agent, and sold his more recent home by himself. "One of the biggest hassles was having to take on the role of both the seller and the agent. It meant that I had to handle everything from scheduling viewings and open houses, to negotiating with buyers, to handling all the paperwork.

"I also had to deal with the emotional aspect of selling our home, which was not easy. It was hard to detach myself from the sentimental value of our home and to be objective when negotiating with potential buyers.

Also, the legal aspects of selling a home can be overwhelming. There were many forms to fill out and deadlines to meet, and it was difficult to keep track of everything. Selling a home yourself is not for the faint of heart. It requires a lot of time, effort and dedication."

Reality check

OK, we're really excited about the possibility of saving a ton of money by selling your home yourself. But the cold fact is that most people who go the FSBO route fail. The reason? They don't study up on the process ahead of time. They try to learn as they go along, and that doesn't cut it. Would you try to pilot an airplane before taking flying lessons? I don't think so—unless you have a death wish.

In fact, For Sale by Owner properties usually take longer to sell, and they sell for way less money than properties handled by an agent – up to 10 percent less. So most FSBOs end up losing money because they didn't do a good job—and they tend to lose way more money than if they had hired a real estate agent to take care of the whole thing! Fortunately, after following the advice in this book, you'll be a pro!

Why exactly do most FSBOs fail? For starters, most of them just aren't prepared for the amount of work that goes into selling a house without professional help. Sure, you might save a lot of money you would have paid in commissions, but you also have to do a lot more legwork.

The number one task in selling real estate is pricing and listing your home correctly. Pricing a property correctly is crucial for a successful sale because it can make the difference between a property sitting on the market for an extended period of time or selling quickly. Pricing the property too high can turn off potential buyers, while pricing it too low can result in leaving money on the table. A good real estate agent or appraiser can provide a professional opinion on the right price and help to list the property accordingly. Additionally, the agent or appraiser can help to market the property effectively to potential buyers, by showcasing the property's best features and highlighting its unique selling points.

And that's not all, folks!

Selling a home isn't like a bowl of cherries, it's a grind. Let's begin:

- Determine the fair market value of your home.
- Prepare your home for sale by making necessary repairs and improvements.
- Create a listing for your home on various online platforms.
- Take high-quality photos of your home.
- Create and illustrate a floor plan of your home.
- Write a list of features and upgrades of your home.
- Advertise your home through various channels (e.g., social media, local classifieds, etc., online platforms like Zillow and Redfin).
- Schedule and conduct open houses or private showings of your home.
- Respond to inquiries from potential buyers.
- Negotiate offers and counteroffers with buyers.

- Review and complete all necessary paperwork for the sale.
- Coordinate with a closing agent, attorney, or escrow company to handle the closing process.
- Obtain any necessary inspections or certifications (e.g., home inspection, radon test, etc.).
- Coordinate the move-out process with the buyers.
- Ensure all necessary paperwork is completed and filed correctly.

Sounds like a lot, huh? We'll cover all these topics in this book, and then some.

The most important mistake most FSBO s make is they price their homes way too high. They think that because they've put a lot of money and effort into their home, it must be worth more than it actually is. But buyers don't care how much you've invested in your home, it doesn't matter to them if you've sunk a million dollars into it. They care only about what similar homes in the area are selling for, and how your home stacks up against the competition.

If you price your home too high, it's going to end up sitting on the market for months and months, with no bites. And the longer your house sits on the market, the less likely it will ever sell. Online, buyers can see how many days your home is on the market. And if your home sits there for three weeks without an offer, that's a red flag that something is wrong (and usually it's the price).

Just because your neighbor down the street sold their place last year for $500,000 does not necessarily you're your house will sell for the same price. The market probably will have changed by now – maybe it's gone up, maybe it's gone down. It's your task to find out, and adjust your strategy accordingly.

Another big mistake people make is not preparing their home for showings. You wouldn't believe some of the horror stories I've heard: homes with dirty dishes piled high in the sink. Piles of unwashed laundry everywhere, and even a dead mouse in the corner (yuck!). That's not just gross, it's a huge turn off for potential buyers. They need to be able to picture themselves living in the house, and they won't want to picture living in a pigsty. So, figure out if you need to clean up, declutter, and make any necessary repairs before you start showing your home.

And then there's the marketing. A lot of people think that just because they've listed their home online, buyers will come flooding in. But that's just not how it works. You have to put in the effort to market your home to potential buyers. And that doesn't just mean listing it on a few websites. More about this later.

And it's not just about the preparation and marketing, it's also about the negotiation. It's like trying to bargain with a car salesman, it can be a daunting task. A lot of people don't realize that they need to be prepared to negotiate with potential buyers. And if you're not familiar with the process, it can be pretty overwhelming. And even if you're confident in your negotiation skills, you might still be at a disadvantage when you're up against a seasoned agent. We will cover the task of negotiating later, in more detail.

The good news is, every mistake you might make in selling your house is completely avoidable.

Another mistake that many homeowners make is not researching the legal and financial aspects of selling a home. This includes things like filling out the necessary paperwork, understanding the closing process, and dealing with title and escrow. Not having a complete understanding of these aspects can lead to delays and even legal issues down the line. It's important to seek professional guidance, such as consulting a real estate attorney, if you have any doubts or concerns.

Another mistake that homeowners make when trying to sell their home without an agent is not being realistic about their expectations. Selling a home is not a quick process, it's like dating—it takes time and effort. Not every potential buyer will be interested in your home. It's important to have realistic expectations and be prepared for the process to take longer than expected.

Don't ignore the legal stuff

This is where you can really get stuck in the much: legal stuff. When it comes to selling your house without a real estate agent, it's important to understand that there are still local laws and regulations that you need to abide by. I've seen firsthand how not doing your research can lead to legal headaches and financial losses. These laws and regulations can vary from state to state, so it's important to do your research and understand the specific requirements in your area.

One of the most important things to understand is your state's laws regarding disclosing any known defects in the home. I've seen how failure to disclose known defects can lead to legal issues down the line. This means that as the seller, you are legally required to disclose any issues with the home that you are aware of, such as a leaky roof, a flooding basement, or a faulty foundation. Some sellers get caught for not disclosing known defects and ended up paying a hefty fine. It's important to be upfront and honest about any issues with the home, even if it might make the sale less attractive. Trust me, it's better to be honest from the start to avoid any legal issues down the line.

Another important aspect to consider is making sure all the necessary paperwork is in order. This includes things like the title and deed to the property, as well as any necessary disclosures and contracts. It's important to have all these documents in order before listing the home, to avoid any delays or complications during the sale process.

Additionally, you will also want to be aware of any local regulations regarding property taxes, zoning and building codes, and other regulations that might apply to your specific property. These regulations can affect the value of your property, and failure to comply with them might lead to penalties or legal issues.

Be aware of any local bylaws, rules and regulations that might affect the sale process. This includes understanding the rules surrounding open houses, signs and advertising, and any other regulations that might apply to your area.

It's helpful to seek legal advice, especially when it comes to drawing up contracts and agreements with potential buyers. A lawyer can help ensure that all the paperwork is in order and that you are protected in case of any legal disputes.

It's also important to be aware of the closing process and what to expect when selling your home without a real estate agent. This includes understanding the role of title and escrow companies, how to handle the transfer of funds, and what to expect during the final closing.

Here's where FSBOs fail

So we've learned that For Sale by Owner might be more of a hassle than you think. Let's look in more detail and the most common downfalls of FSBOs. ...And the nominations for the most common and costly screw-ups are:

Mistake #1: Pricing your home too high

One of the most common mistakes homeowners make when selling their house without a realtor is pricing it too high. It's natural to want to get the most money possible for your home, but setting the price too high can actually hurt your chances of selling it. Potential buyers will be deterred by the high price and may not even bother looking at your home. Additionally, if your home is on the market for too long, buyers may start to wonder if there's something wrong with it.

To avoid this mistake, do your research and find out what similar homes in your area have sold for. This will give you an idea of what to expect when it comes to pricing your home. And, when in doubt, it's always better to price your home slightly lower than you think it's worth. This will help attract more potential buyers and increase the chances of a sale.

I remember when I first put my first home on the market, I had this idea that it was worth more than it actually was. In retrospect, that was just wishful thinking. I priced it way too high, thinking that buyers would just come flocking to my door, because I thought my house was more special than any other house in the area. I didn't get a single offer and it sat on the market for months. It was a tough pill to swallow, but eventually, I had to accept that it was priced too high and lower the price to something more reasonable.

It was a hard lesson to learn, but it taught me the importance of pricing your home correctly. Pricing your home too high can be a huge mistake, as it can discourage buyers from even viewing it and it can lead to a longer time on the market. It's important to research comparable homes in your area, and to consult with a real estate agent to get an accurate idea of what your home is worth. Trust me, it's better to price it a little lower and get multiple offers (which can lead to a bidding war among buyers) than to price it too high and have it sit on the market for months.

Mistake #2: Skimping on home staging

Another mistake homeowners make when selling their house without a realtor is skimping on home staging. Home staging is the process of preparing your home for sale by making it look as attractive as possible to potential buyers. This can include decluttering, rearranging furniture, and making repairs or updates to the home. We'll look at staging in more detail later.

Now, I know some of you may be thinking, "Why spend all that money and effort on staging when I can just plop a "for sale" sign in the yard and call it a day?" Showing without making the effort of staging is like trying to sell a car without washing it first. Sure, it might still sell, but it's not going to fetch the best price.

Make sure that your home is presented at its best, and it will sell faster and for a higher price.

Even if your home isn't staged to the max, there's still a lot you can do to help its appearance. Take the time to declutter and depersonalize your home before showings. This can include removing personal photos, excess furniture, and any other items that may distract from the features of the home. Additionally, make sure to keep the home clean and tidy, as this will help create a positive impression on potential buyers.

Mistake #3: Lackluster marketing

A third mistake homeowners make when selling their house without a realtor is not marketing it effectively. A good realtor will have a marketing plan in place to help sell your home, but when you're selling on your own, it's up to you to get the word out.

Make sure to list your home on all the major real estate websites, such as Zillow and Realtor.com. Additionally, consider using social media platforms to promote your home and reach a wider audience. And, don't be afraid to reach out to your personal network and ask them to spread the word about your home for sale.

By avoiding these common mistakes, you'll increase your chances of selling your home quickly and for the best price possible. Remember, selling a house without a realtor can be a bit more challenging, but with a bit of effort and preparation, it can be done.

Mistake #4: Not being available for showings

Another mistake homeowners make when selling their house without a realtor is not being available for showings. When you're working with a realtor, they'll handle the scheduling of showings and make sure your home is available for potential buyers to view. But when you're selling on your own, it's up to you to make sure your home is accessible and ready to be shown.

And if you're not available to show your home to potential buyers when it's convenient for them, it's like flushing opportunities down the toilet. Be flexible with your schedule and make sure you're available for showings at a moment's notice. This can be difficult if you have a busy schedule or if you're still living in the home while it's on the market. But, it's important to remember that the more accessible your home is for showings, the greater the chances of making a sale.

Just remember, the more accessible your home is for showings, the greater the chances of making a sale, and before you know it, you'll be handing over the keys to your new home and enjoying your own little vacation in a new place.

Mistake #5: Not disclosing known issues

We've hammered on this before, but it's worth hearing again: one of the biggest mistakes homeowners make when selling their house without a realtor is not disclosing known issues with the home. As a seller, you're required by law to disclose any known defects or issues with your home to potential buyers. Failing to do so can lead to legal issues and can even jeopardize the sale.

It's important to be upfront and honest about any issues with your home, even if they seem minor. This can include things like a leaky roof, foundation problems, or any other issues that may affect the structural integrity of the home. By disclosing these issues, you'll help potential buyers make an informed decision and avoid any surprises down the line.

Mistake #7: Not knowing the paperwork and legalities

Finally, another mistake homeowners make when selling their house without a realtor is not knowing the paperwork and legalities involved. Selling a house without a realtor can be a bit more challenging, but with a bit of effort and preparation, it can be done. However, it is important to know the legal and paperwork process that goes with selling the house. From drafting the sales contract to the transfer of ownership and mortgage, not being familiar with the legal requirements can cause delays and even jeopardize the sale.

To avoid this mistake, it is advisable to seek legal advice and assistance to ensure that everything is in order and that all legal requirements are met. This can save you a lot of time, money, and stress in the long run.

Mistake #9: Not being prepared for negotiations

Another mistake homeowners make when selling their house without a realtor is not being prepared for negotiations. Selling a house without a realtor can be a bit more challenging, but with a bit of effort and preparation, it can be done. However, it is important to be prepared for negotiations and to have a good understanding of the process.

To avoid this mistake, it is advisable to have a clear understanding of your bottom line, what you are willing to accept, and what you are not willing to accept. It is also important to be prepared to compromise and understand the buyer's perspective. This can help to make the negotiation process smoother, and will increase the chances of making a sale.

Mistake #10: Not considering the cost of selling

Another mistake homeowners make when selling their house without a realtor is not considering the cost of selling. When you sell your home with the help of a realtor, they will typically charge a commission, which can be a significant expense. However, when you sell your home on your own, you will still have costs associated with the sale, such as closing costs, legal fees, and advertising expenses.

To avoid this mistake, it's important to do your research and understand the costs associated with selling your home on your own. Make sure to budget for these expenses and factor them into your asking price. This will help ensure that you don't end up losing money on the sale.

One way to make the process of selling your home without a realtor more financially manageable is by working with a flat-fee listing service. These services provide homeowners with the tools and resources needed to sell their home on their own, but at a fraction of the cost of a traditional realtor.

In conclusion, selling a house without a realtor can be a daunting task, but with proper preparation and knowledge, it can be done. Remember, by avoiding these common mistakes, you'll increase your chances of selling your home quickly and for the best price possible. And most importantly, you will be able to sell your home with confidence and peace of mind.

Know your competition

OK, our next tasks: determining your home's market value. Well, let me tell you, it's all about researching comparable sales in your area and understanding the current state of the housing market. And don't worry, it's not as complicated as it sounds, I'll walk you through it step by step.

First things first, you need to start by gathering information about comparable sales in your area. This means looking at houses that are similar to yours in terms of size, age, location, and condition. Websites like Zillow and Redfin are great resources for this information, and you can also check your local real estate listings for more information. Once you've gathered all this information, you'll be able to get a pretty good idea of how much houses like yours are selling for in your area. And trust me, it's a lot more fun than it sounds, you'll be surprised at how much you'll learn about your neighborhood and local market.

But it's not just about comparable sales, you also need to take into account the current state of the housing market. Are you in a buyer's market or a seller's market? In a buyer's market, buyers have the upper hand, they can demand a discount from your asking price, and demand other concessions. In a seller's market, you might be able to price your home a little higher, and potential buyers might even offer more than your asking price.

It's also important to consider any unique features or selling points of your home, such as new appliances, recent renovations, or a desirable location. These factors can add value to your home and should be taken into account when determining your home's market value.

Now, I know what you might be thinking, "It sounds like a lot of work, do I really have to do all of this?" And the answer is yes. Determining your home's market value is essential to the success of your sale and will pay off in the end. As a wise soul once said, "Price it right and it will sell overnight, price it wrong and it will sit forever."

If you're not sure of your home's value, get a professional opinion. Reach out to a local real estate appraiser and have them give you an estimate of your home's value. This will be a great way to get a professional and unbiased opinion on your home's value. The appraiser will take into account all the same factors you considered, such as comparable sales and the current state of the housing market, but they will also have access to more detailed information and data. We'll cover real estate appraisals in more detail later.

You can also reach out to local real estate agents to get their opinions on your home's value, which would not be as accurate as a report from a licensed appraiser, but would be pretty accurate. As I've said before, no good real estate will refuse to chat with you about the business – they love talking about it!

Another tip that can be useful is to walk around your neighborhood and check out open houses for homes similar to yours. This will give you a chance to see how other sellers are presenting and pricing their homes, and it will also help you understand what features and amenities buyers are looking for in a home.

It's also important to consider any unique features or selling points of your home, such as new appliances, recent renovations, or a desirable location. These factors can add value to your home and should be taken into account when pricing your home.

"When we decided to put our beloved home on the market, we knew that pricing it accurately would be key," said Paul. "We dove headfirst into researching the current market conditions, utilizing various online resources and speaking with local real estate experts to gain a thorough understanding of the value of our home.

We meticulously examined the recent sales of similar homes in the area, taking into account factors such as the size, condition and location of the home, as well as the current market trends and demand.

"Then we carefully crafted a pricing strategy that would be both fair and effective. We determined a range of prices *that our home could sell for and decided on a listing price that we felt was most suitable.*

"Fortunately, our home sold quickly, and for a price that exceeded our expectations. We couldn't be happier with the outcome and realized that pricing our home accurately was the essential factor in getting the best return on our investment."

Be strategic with your pricing. You can start by pricing your home slightly higher than what you expect to get, and then gradually lower the price if you don't get any bites. This is known as the "anchoring" technique, and it can help you get closer to your desired price.

An alternate strategy would be to price your home a little lower than you believe the market price is. In a strong sellers' market, this could result in a bidding war among buyers, pushing their offers way above your asking price.

It's also important to be flexible when it comes to pricing your home. Be prepared to negotiate with buyers and be open to offers. You might not get your asking price, but if you're flexible, you'll be more likely to find a buyer and close the sale.

Pricing your home too high might drive away potential buyers, who are looking for a good deal. You'll also miss out on buyers who are looking for homes in your price range. On the other hand, pricing your home too low might result in you leaving money on the table. So it's important to find a balance and price your home competitively.

Another important tip is to be aware of the seasonality of the housing market. Spring and summer are typically considered the best time to sell, as the weather is nicer and more buyers are looking to purchase a home. However, it's important to be aware of the local market trends in your area, as it may vary.

Ready, set ...

Before you start showing your house to potential buyers, there are a few things you should do to make sure it's in its best condition. In this chapter, we'll cover some specific tips for staging and preparing your home for showings, such as decluttering, neutralizing colors, and making necessary repairs.

Decluttering

You're about to take the first step in getting your house in top-notch condition for potential buyers—that means getting rid of stuff stacked up on countertops, in corners, and spilling off bookshelves. But before you start, it's important to understand that decluttering is not just about getting rid of stuff, it's about creating a space that feels open, spacious, and inviting. In this chapter, I'll share some tips for decluttering your home, including setting a goal, creating a plan, and staying motivated. I'll also share my own personal experiences and anecdotes to help you through this process.

It can seem like an endless task at first, but start by setting a manageable goal. Have a clear idea of what you want to accomplish. I recommend making a list of specific areas in your home that you want to declutter and setting a deadline for when you want to have it done. When I first started decluttering, my goal was to get rid of 50 items per day and it really helped me stay focused and motivated. Another person I know had a goal to declutter her garage in a month, and she did it with flying colors. As the saying goes, "A goal without a deadline is just a dream." So, set a goal and use it to motivate you.

Next, let's talk about creating a plan. Once you've set a goal, it's time to create a plan on how you're going to achieve it. This includes things like setting a schedule, creating a checklist, and identifying problem areas. For example, you can schedule a specific day and time each week to declutter a room or create a checklist of items you want to get rid of. Also, it's important to identify problem areas in your home that tend to accumulate clutter, such as the kitchen counter or the bedroom dresser. In my own experience, I found that my home office was a problem area and I was able to declutter it by getting rid of items I no longer needed. As the famous motivational speaker, Tony Robbins, says, "A goal without a plan is just a wish." Therefore, have a clear plan in place to make decluttering more manageable.

Keep going!

Now that we've covered setting a goal and creating a plan, let's talk about staying motivated. Decluttering can be a daunting task, and it's easy to lose steam along the way. To stay motivated, it's important to remember why you're doing it in the first place. Whether it's to sell your house for a better price or to create a more peaceful living space, keep your end goal in mind. In my own experience, I found that setting small milestones along the way helped me stay motivated. For example, after decluttering a room, I would take a break and celebrate the accomplishment before moving on to the next one. Also, try to make decluttering a fun and rewarding experience by listening to music or inviting a friend to help.

Getting rid of your junk can be the hardest part of decluttering, but it's also the most important. When deciding what objects to keep and what to get rid of, ask yourself if the item brings you joy, if you use it regularly, or if it has sentimental value. If the answer is no, let it go. Otherwise, that stuff is like an albatross around your neck. In my own experience, I found that it helped to have a designated "getting rid of" area in my home where I would place items I no longer needed. Be ruthless in your decluttering and get rid of items that no longer serve a purpose.

Happy decluttering!

Sara had decided to sell her home without a real estate agent. She had lived in the house for many years and had accumulated a lot of clutter over time. She knew that in order to get the best price for her house, she would need to declutter it first.

"I know that in order to sell my house for the best price, I need to declutter it first. But where do I even begin? It feels overwhelming," Sara said.

A friend suggested that she start by tackling one room at a time. She also recommended that Sara focus on getting rid of items she no longer needed or used.

Sara: "You're right. I'll start with one room at a time and focus on getting rid of things I no longer need or use."

Sara began by decluttering her living room. She went through her bookshelves and got rid of any books she had already read and didn't need to keep. She also went through her collection of knick-knacks and got rid of anything that was just taking up space. She donated to charity clothes, books, and other items that were still in good condition (which can be a tax deduction).

"I can't believe how much better my living room looks already," she said. " I have so much more space and it looks more open and inviting. It's amazing what a difference getting rid of clutter can make. The room feels bigger and brighter and I'm sure potential buyers will be able to envision themselves living here."

Sara then moved on to her bedroom, where she went through her closet and got rid of any clothes she hadn't worn in a while. She also went through her nightstands and got rid of any old magazines or papers that she no longer needed. She also removed any extra furniture that was taking up space in the room.

"My bedroom looks so much better now," Sara said. "It's more spacious and it's easier to focus on the features of the

room that I want to highlight, like the large windows and the hardwood floors."

Sara continued this process throughout the rest of her house, decluttering each room one by one. She found that it was not only helpful for selling her house but also for her mental well-being.

"I feel like a weight has been lifted off my shoulders, and I'm sure potential buyers will appreciate how well-maintained and organized my house looks."

By decluttering her house, Sara was able to make it more attractive to potential buyers and ultimately, sell her home at the price she was looking for, without the help of a real estate agent.

Color your world

Next, let's talk about neutralizing colors. This doesn't mean you have to paint your entire house beige, but it does mean you should avoid bold or bright colors that might turn off potential buyers. If your daughter's room was painted hot pink, it might be a great memory for you, but not a great selling point for most buyers. Stick to neutral colors that will appeal to a wide range of people. This will make it easier for buyers to envision themselves living in your home. "Neutral colors are the perfect background for strong architectural statements, and can act as a foil for interesting textures and patterns," says designer Michael S. Smith.

Neutral colors also make your home look more spacious and open, which can be a major selling point.

Neutral colors are the little black dress of home decorating, they never go out of style.

This is how we do it

OK, we've decided to neutralize, but exactly how do we do it? The first step is to identify the areas that need to be neutralized. This can include walls, furniture, and accessories. Next, choose a color palette of neutral colors such as beige, gray, or taupe. These colors are easy to work with and can be paired with any other color. Once you have your color palette, it's time to start neutralizing. This can include painting walls, replacing bold colored furniture with neutral colored pieces, and swapping out colorful accessories with neutral ones. When I was selling my own home, I painted the walls an eggshell color, replaced my brightly colored throw pillows with neutral ones, and removed any personal items with bold colors. This helped make the space feel more open and welcoming to potential buyers.

It's also important to keep in mind that neutralizing colors doesn't mean you have to completely get rid of color in your home. You can still add pops of color through artwork, plants, and other accessories. But keep in mind that these items should be easily removable and not too bold. Neutral colors don't necessarily mean boring, it's all about finding the right balance.

Another tip is to consider the lighting in your home. Natural light can enhance the colors in your home and make them appear brighter or bolder. But, when you're trying to neutralize the colors, you might want to consider partially closing curtains or blinds during showings to make the colors appear more neutral. But don't shut out too much light, and make your entire house look like a dungeon.

Another tip for neutralizing colors is to focus on the main living areas of your home. The living room, dining room, and kitchen are the spaces where potential buyers will spend the most time, so it's important to make sure these areas are neutralized. This includes walls, furniture, and accessories. For example, if you have a bold colored accent wall in your living room, consider painting it a neutral color. If you have a colorful couch or dining table, consider covering it with a neutral colored slipcover or replacing it with a neutral colored piece. And, if you have colorful accessories such as blankets or curtains, consider swapping them out for neutral colored ones.

Sometimes, it's the small things that make a big difference. For example, if you have bold colored knobs or handles on your kitchen cabinets, consider replacing them with neutral colored ones. Or, if you have a colorful rug in your living room, consider replacing it with a neutral colored one. These small changes can make a big impact in neutralizing the colors in your home.

I found that neutralizing the colors in my home was a simple but effective way to make it more appealing to potential buyers. It made the space feel more open and welcoming. Remember, neutralizing colors is not about completely getting rid of color, it's about finding the right balance. So, use these tips to neutralize the colors in your home and make it more appealing to potential buyers.

Another thing to keep in mind when neutralizing colors is to focus on creating a cohesive look throughout your home. This means choosing a color palette and sticking to it throughout the entire house. For example, you might choose a neutral color palette that includes shades of beige, gray, and taupe. Then, use these colors consistently throughout your home in walls, furniture, and accessories. This will help create a cohesive look that makes your home feel more put together and polished.

Also, it pays to consider the style of your home when choosing neutral colors. For example, if your home has a traditional style, you might choose more classic neutral colors such as beige or gray. On the other hand, if your home has a modern style, you might choose more contemporary neutral colors such as white or black. The key is to choose colors that complement the style of your home and make it feel more polished and cohesive.

Repairs: no fun, but must be done

Now that we've covered decluttering and neutralizing colors, let's talk about making necessary repairs. Many sellers overlook this step, but ignoring this step can sabotage the sale of your home. Buyers will notice signs of neglect or disrepair. Fixing these issues before showing your house will give buyers the impression that your home has been well-cared for. This will increase their confidence in the purchase and help you get a better price.

In this chapter, I'll share some tips on how to make necessary repairs in your home, including why it's important, how to do it, how much it will cost and my own personal examples and experiences.

The first step is to identify which repairs are necessary. This can include things like fixing leaky faucets, repairing cracks in walls or floors, and replacing old light fixtures. Next, create a list of the repairs that need to be made and prioritize them by urgency. This will help you focus on the most important repairs first. Once you have a list of repairs, it's time to start making them. Some repairs you may be able to do yourself, but for others, you may need to hire a professional. I always recommend getting multiple quotes and checking references before hiring a professional. Also, it's important to have a budget and stick to it. Making necessary repairs can be costly, so it's important to have a plan in place to keep costs under control.

Let's talk about the elephant in the room: cost. We all know that making necessary repairs can come with a pretty hefty price tag. But, before you start getting sticker shock, remember that these repairs can lead to a higher sale price and a quicker sale. So, when creating your budget for repairs, make sure to include a buffer for unexpected costs. Trust me, I've learned the hard way that it's better to overestimate the cost of repairs than to underestimate it. That way, you'll be prepared for any unexpected expenses and won't be left with a surprise bill.

Another tip is to focus on repairs that will have the biggest impact. For example, fixing a leaky faucet or replacing old light fixtures might not cost a lot, but they can make a big difference in the overall appearance of your home. On the other hand, a major renovation such as a kitchen remodel can be costly, but it can also have a big impact on the value of your home. So, focus on making repairs that will have the biggest impact for the least amount of cost. I like to think of it as a game of 'Bang for your Buck'. And remember, a little bit of elbow grease and a few dollars can go a long way in making your home more appealing to potential buyers."

It's also important to keep in mind that making necessary repairs is not just about fixing things that are broken, it's also about making sure everything is in good working condition. This can include things like cleaning gutters, testing smoke detectors, and checking for any drafts. These small repairs may not cost a lot, but they can make a big difference in the overall appearance of your home and show potential buyers that your home has been well-maintained.

If your gutters are clogged, it can cause water to overflow and damage your home. I learned this from my own experience, when I was getting ready to sell my home, I realized that my gutters were clogged and it had caused water damage to my home, so I had to clean them before listing my home.

Another tip is to consider the timing of repairs. If you're planning to sell your home in the near future, it's best to make repairs before listing your home. This will save you time and money, and it will also make your home more appealing to potential buyers. However, if you're not planning to sell your home soon, you may want to consider making repairs as they are needed. This will help you avoid costly repairs in the future and keep your home in good working condition.

Lastly, another common household repair that is often ignored is checking for drafts. Drafts can cause your energy bills to be higher and make your home less comfortable to live in. I realized this from my own experience, when I was getting ready to sell my home, I noticed that some of the windows and doors were drafty, so I had to seal them before listing my home.

In conclusion, making necessary repairs is an important step in preparing your home for showings. It can increase the value of your home, make it more appealing to potential buyers, and can lead to a quicker sale and a higher price. Remember to identify which repairs are necessary, prioritize them by urgency, consider the cost, timing, and safety and make your home a comfortable and safe place to live. Happy repairing!

All your home is a stage

OK, let's take things to the next level: making your home look inviting for visitors. This includes things like making sure the house is clean, adding some fresh flowers, and making sure the temperature is comfortable. These small touches can make a big difference in how buyers perceive your home. As the great American author Maya Angelou said, "People will forget what you said, people will forget what you did, but people will never forget how you made them feel." So, make sure your home feels inviting and welcoming to potential buyers.

For example, focus on lighting. Good lighting can make a big difference in the overall appearance of your home. Consider adding lamps or new light fixtures to brighten up your home. Natural light can also make a big difference, so make sure to keep curtains and blinds open during showings. When I was selling my own home, I added new light fixtures and made sure to keep the curtains open to let in natural light, which helped make the space feel more open and inviting.

Staging

Staging your home means making it as good as you can, no matter what it looks like now. It's the process of turning your home into a model home to make it more appealing to potential buyers. Think of it like a makeover for your house. In this chapter, I'll share some tips on how to stage your home, including why it's important, how to do it, and how to get help doing it. And trust me, I've got plenty of personal anecdotes and experiences to share with you.

First, let's talk about why staging your home is important. It's like putting your best foot forward when meeting someone new. Staging your home can make it more appealing to potential buyers. It can make your home look more spacious, open, and welcoming. It can also help potential buyers envision themselves living in the space. I've seen firsthand how staging can make a big difference in making a home more appealing to potential buyers and how it can lead to a quicker sale and a higher price.

Now, let's talk about how to stage your home. One important aspect of staging is rearranging furniture. This means moving furniture around to make your home look more spacious and open. Try moving larger pieces of furniture to the perimeter of the room and smaller pieces to the center. Also, make sure to remove any furniture that is not necessary. This will make your home look more spacious and open. In my own experience, I found that rearranging furniture helped make my home look more open and welcoming, and it even made my cat more confused about where his bed was."

Another important aspect of staging is adding decor. This can include things like fresh flowers, candles, or a bowl of fruit. These small touches can make a big difference in making your home look more inviting. In my own experience, I found that adding decor helped make my home look more polished and attractive.

"When we sold our home, we hired a professional staging consultant to help us prepare our home for potential buyers," said Anne. "The staging consultant came to our home and gave us a detailed report on what we needed to do to make it more attractive to buyers. She suggested that we declutter and depersonalize the space, rearrange furniture, and update some of the decor. She gave us a detailed report on what we needed to do to make our home more attractive to buyers, she suggested that we declutter, depersonalize the space, rearrange furniture, and update some of the decor. She offered to completely redecorate the house with her company's furniture, if we wanted to put our items in temporary storage.

We made the changes she suggested. We decluttered and removed personal items, rearranged the furniture to make the space feel more open and inviting, and added some new decor to give the house a fresh look. It was amazing to see how much of a difference it made to the house, it looked more open and inviting and the fresh decor added a new look to the space.

Our staging consultant also helped us to set up the home for showings. She made sure that everything was in its place and that the home was ready for potential buyers to come in and see."

It certainly helps to get professional help staging your home, but if you're on a tight budget, you can also try to stage your home yourself. Websites like Pinterest and Houzz can provide you with great ideas on how to stage your home.

Another way to get help with staging your home is to ask for the opinion of friends or family members. They can provide you with an objective point of view and can help you identify areas of your home that need improvement.

It's also important to keep in mind that staging is not just about making your home look good, it's also about making it feel good. This means paying attention to the atmosphere of your home, the lighting and the smell. Try to create a warm and welcoming atmosphere by lighting scented candles, or adding a fresh scent to your home. This can help create a positive and inviting feeling for potential buyers. When you live in a place you can become immune to its smell. And if the smell isn't good, it's a huge turnoff for buyers.

In addition, pay attention to the small details, like making sure that your home is clean and tidy, that all the light bulbs are working, and that the house is well-ventilated. These small details can make a big difference in creating a positive atmosphere and can help attract potential buyers.

De-personalizing your home is an important step in preparing it for sale. It involves removing any personal items such as family photos, religious artifacts, and other personal belongings that may make it difficult for potential buyers to envision themselves living in the space. This can include items such as family heirlooms, sentimental trinkets, and personal artwork. By removing these items, you can create a neutral and inviting space that appeals to a wider range of potential buyers.

For example, family photos or personal art can be replaced with neutral wall decor such as landscapes or abstract art. You can also remove any personal items from the kitchen, such as family photos or magnets from the fridge, and replace them with neutral items such as herbs or a vase of flowers. Personalized items in the bedrooms should also be removed, such as family photos on nightstands or headboards.

It's also important to remove any religious artifacts or symbols that may not be in line with the beliefs of potential buyers. This can include items such as crosses, religious statues, or other religious decor.

De-personalizing your home can be difficult, but it's important to remember that it's only temporary and it will help you sell your home faster and for a better price. If you need help deciding what to remove, you can ask a real estate agent or a home stager for their opinion. They will be able to give you a better idea of what needs to be removed to make your home more appealing to potential buyers.

I know it can be tough to hide your beloved family photos and personal trinkets, but trust me, it's for a good cause. Think of it like a makeover for your home. You're making it desirable to the biggest cross-section of homebuyers, and that means you'll be able to sell your home faster and at the best price. And who doesn't want to sell their home faster and for more money?

It may feel like you're stripping your home of its personality and character, but let's be real, potential buyers don't want to see your vacation photos from 1999 or that weird sculpture you got at a garage sale. They want to envision themselves living in the space, and that's hard to do with your personal artifacts everywhere.

Where the buffalo roam ...

In addition to neutralizing colors and de-personalizing your home, it's also important to create a sense of flow throughout the home. This means that you should create a clear path for potential buyers to walk through the home and make sure that each room flows seamlessly into the next. This can be achieved by removing any unnecessary furniture or items that can block the flow of traffic.

Another important aspect of staging your home is to create an illusion of space. This can be achieved by removing any unnecessary furniture, and by creating a sense of flow throughout the home. Additionally, you can create the illusion of space by using mirrors and by adding light-colored rugs or curtains that can help reflect light and make the space feel bigger.

Another important aspect of staging your home is to make sure it shows well in photos and videos, as these will be the first impression that many potential buyers will have of your home. Make sure that your home is well-lit, and that any clutter or personal items are removed before taking photos or videos. Also, consider hiring a professional photographer or videographer, as they will have the necessary equipment and skills to make your home look its best.

Is it really worth hiring a professional photographer? You might say, "Well, I have an excellent camera on my phone, and I can take dozens of pictures and video in 10 minutes, and it won't cost me a cent." Well, consider this: Any real estate agent worth their salt hires a professional photographer for the homes they're selling, and why do you think they do it? It's not because they enjoy wasting money. It's because they have learned through experience that professional photos will make your house look much better on websites and in printed materials, making it more likely that the house will sell quickly at the highest price possible.

A professional photographer has the necessary equipment and skills to make your home look its best in photos and videos. They know how to use lighting and angles to make your home look more attractive and spacious. They can also help you stage your home to make it more appealing to potential buyers. Consider spending a couple hundred bucks for professional photos.

How to stage your home if it's empty

Maybe you've already moved, and your house is unoccupied—no furniture, not even a lawn chair. How do you stage your home now?

Staging an unoccupied home for sale can be a bit more involved than staging an occupied home, but with the right approach, it's still possible to make it look attractive to potential buyers. Here are a few tips on how to stage an unoccupied home for sale:

Add furniture: If the home is empty, it's important to add furniture to make it look more lived-in. This can be done by renting furniture or by using your own furniture if you have any that is not currently in use.

Use decor to create a cohesive look: Use decor to create a cohesive look throughout the home. This includes using similar color schemes, textures, and styles in each room. This will help potential buyers to envision themselves living in the space.

Use lighting to create ambiance: Lighting can play a big role in creating an inviting atmosphere in an unoccupied home. Use a variety of lighting sources, such as table lamps and floor lamps, to create a warm and welcoming ambiance.

Highlight the home's best features: Use decor and lighting to highlight the home's best features, such as large windows, hardwood floors, or a beautiful fireplace.

Keep the home in "show-ready" condition: Even when the home is not being shown, it's important to keep it in "show-ready" condition. This means making sure it's always clean, tidy, and well-maintained. It's also important to keep the temperature and lighting in the home consistent.

Another must is paying attention to the curb appeal of your home. This means making sure that the outside of your home is well-maintained and looks attractive. This can include things like mowing the lawn, trimming bushes, and planting flowers. A well-maintained exterior can make a big difference in attracting potential buyers and can also increase the value of your home.

In addition, it's important to consider the needs and preferences of your target audience when staging your home. For example, if you're targeting families with young children, make sure that your home is child-friendly and safe. If you're targeting older buyers, make sure that your home is accessible and easy to navigate.

Preparing your home for showings takes a little bit of effort, but it's worth it in the end. By decluttering, neutralizing colors, making necessary repairs, and making your home look inviting, you'll increase the chances of selling your house quickly and for a good price. Remember, as the famous real estate mogul, Donald Trump, says, "The best deals are made when both parties walk away feeling like they've won." So, make sure your home is in its best condition and you'll be on your way to a successful sale."

Marketing and advertising

Marketing is a crucial aspect of selling your house without a realtor. In this chapter, we'll take a look at the best ways to market your home online and offline. By understanding the different marketing strategies available to you, you'll be able to create a marketing plan that will help you sell your home quickly and for the best price possible.

Publicizing an open house used to be pretty simple: you just placed a little ad in your local Sunday newspaper. But a little newspaper ad doesn't cut it anymore.

Today, it's essential to list your home on the big home-search sites such as Zillow, Redfin, and Trulia that allow you to list your home for free or for a small fee. When you create a FSBO listing, you'll be able to upload pictures, videos, and a detailed description of your home, and potential buyers will be able to contact you directly.

In addition to listing your home on popular real estate platforms, you can also use social media to market your home. Platforms like Facebook, Instagram, and Twitter are great ways to reach a large audience and increase the visibility of your home. You can create a social media page for your home, post pictures and videos, and share information about the home and neighborhood. This will not only increase the visibility of your home but also create an online community around it.

"Social media is like having a virtual open house, it allows potential buyers to see your home and the lifestyle it offers, even if they're not physically there," says real estate expert Gary Keller.

Open your doors

Another great way to market your home is by hosting open houses. Open houses allow potential buyers to see your home in person, and it also gives them a sense of the lifestyle that comes with your home.

Additionally, holding an open house can also help generate buzz and interest in your home, which can lead to more offers and a faster sale. "An open house is like a party for your home, it creates excitement and interest and it can lead to more offers," says real estate expert Brian Buffini.

An open house is an event where a property is open for potential buyers to come and view it. These events are usually scheduled for a specific day and time and are open to the public. They give potential buyers the opportunity to view the property, walk through the rooms, and ask the seller or their realtor any questions about the property. The purpose of an open house is to give potential buyers a chance to see the property in person, which can help them make a decision about whether to make an offer or not. It also gives the sellers the opportunity to showcase their property to many potential buyers at once.

Open houses allow potential buyers to ask questions about the home and the neighborhood, and it can also give them a sense of the lifestyle that comes with your home.

"An open house is like a sneak peek into the home and the lifestyle it offers, it allows potential buyers to envision themselves living in the home," says real estate expert Barbara Corcoran.

Another important aspect of holding open houses and other showings is having a sign-in sheet. This will allow you to keep track of potential buyers who have visited your home and follow up with them later. An even more effective strategy, if you have the time and inclination, is meeting shoppers at your front door. It's an effective way of gathering their contact information, more reliable than a sign-in sheet. Many visitors won't take the time to complete a sign-in sheet.

Gathering contact information at an open house is important because it allows you to keep in touch with potential buyers who have expressed interest in your property. By having their contact information, you can send them updates about the property, and more information about your house they may have missed during the open house. Additionally, if the property does not sell immediately, you can reach out to them again in the future and let them know if the price has been reduced or if any new developments have occurred.

For example, when I was selling a home, I made sure to gather contact information from all of the attendees at the open house. One of the attendees, a young couple, expressed strong interest in the property, but were not ready to make an offer. I kept in touch with them over the next several days. Eventually, they decided to make an offer on the property, and it was sold successfully. Without gathering their contact information, it would have been impossible to maintain communication with them and I would have missed the opportunity to sell the property to them.

When hosting an open house, it's important to make sure your home is clean and well-lit, and it's also important to have information about the home and the neighborhood available for potential buyers to take with them.

Additionally, it's a good idea to provide refreshments, such as bottled water or cookies, to make potential buyers feel welcome.

"Hosting an open house was a great experience," said Jerry. "As the seller, it was an opportunity to showcase my home to a large number of potential buyers at once. I was able to highlight all the positive features of my home and the surrounding area, and answer any questions that people had.

One of the good things that came out of it was that it helped create a sense of urgency among the potential buyers. They were able to see other people showing interest in my home, which helped push them to make an offer.

"Another good thing was that it gave me valuable feedback about my home. I was able to hear directly from potential buyers about what they liked and didn't like about the house. It helped me to understand what potential buyers were looking for, which I can use to improve my home and make it more attractive to buyers.

"However, there were also some negative things, like the big amount of traffic and strangers in my home. Although it was great to have a lot of people interested in my home, it was also a bit overwhelming to have so many strangers there. I felt like I was constantly tidying up and making sure everything was presentable.

Another irritant was some of the people had no intention of buying, they just wanted to look around. It was a bit frustrating to have to entertain people who weren't really interested in my home."

Have some printed information that shoppers can take with them This can include things like floor plans, neighborhood maps, and school information.

Another effective way to publicize your open house is to print flyers and post them in the neighborhood. This can include things like posting flyers on community bulletin boards, handing out flyers to neighbors, and leaving flyers at local businesses. Additionally, you can print postcards and mail them to potential buyers.

Open houses are a great way to network and connect with potential buyers. This can be especially important when selling your home without a realtor, as it allows potential buyers to get to know you and understand your motivation for selling your home.

Watch what you say

It's important to be available to answer questions from potential buyers and provide information about the home and the neighborhood. Think about this ahead of time, and have a general script ready to use when you meet them and chat.

Now, let's take a look at what to say and what not to say when showing your home to potential buyers. One of the most important things to remember is to be honest about the condition of your home. If there are any issues or repairs that need to be made, it's important to be upfront about them. Additionally, it's a good idea to highlight the positive features of your home, such as recent renovations or upgrades, while avoiding making negative comments about your neighbors or the neighborhood.

Additionally, it's important to be prepared for difficult situations that may arise during open houses or other showings. For example, you may encounter a potential buyer who is difficult to please or who has a lot of questions. In these situations, it's important to remain calm and professional and to be prepared to provide honest and accurate information about your home.

"Be prepared for difficult situations and handle them with grace, it'll show potential buyers that you are a professional and trustworthy seller," says real estate expert Brian Buffini.

"When we decided to put our home on the market, we knew we needed to highlight all the things that made it special," Andy said. "As the seller, I always made sure to point out the updates we had done to the house, like the new flooring and paint. I also talked about the neighborhood and how much we loved it, mentioning things like the convenient location and peaceful streets. I would tell potential buyers, 'Our home has been recently updated with new flooring and paint, and we love the peaceful neighborhood and the convenient location close to shopping and restaurants.

"But I also wanted to be upfront about any issues or potential problems with the house. I would tell them 'The roof is original to the home and will need to be replaced

within the next few years, but we have priced the home accordingly to reflect this.' I knew it was better to be honest about any potential issues with the house rather than have them come up later in the buying process.

"I also made sure not to disclose any personal information about myself or any previous occupants of the home as it is not relevant to the sale and can be considered discriminatory. For example, I've heard you should not volunteer information about a death that occurred in the home, or that a previous occupant had a particular disease.

"In the end, the goal was to present the home in the best possible light, while also being transparent and honest about any potential issues. Thanks to this approach, we were able to find a buyer that fell in love with our home just like we did.

"It was a great feeling to see a potential buyer walk through our home and appreciate all the things that we had loved about it. They were also impressed with how upfront we were about the roof needing to be replaced and appreciated that we had priced the home accordingly.

"It was a smooth process, and I believe that our honest and transparent approach helped build trust with the buyers. They knew they were getting a great home, with no hidden surprises.

"It was definitely a great experience and I would recommend anyone who is selling their home to approach it in the same way. By highlighting the positive features of the property, being honest about any issues, and not disclosing any personal information, you can help make the process as easy and stress-free as possible for everyone involved."

Another key aspect of holding open houses and other showings is to create a sense of ambiance. This can include things like lighting candles or burning scented oils, playing background music, and adjusting the temperature to ensure that the home feels comfortable and inviting.

"Creating a sense of ambiance can help potential buyers feel more at home and make it easier for them to envision themselves living in the space," says real estate expert, Barbara Corcoran.

When planning open houses and other showings, timing is everything. For instance, if you live in an area where the traffic is as heavy as a rush hour in New York City, then holding open houses on weekends might not be the best idea. Instead, try hosting it on a Monday morning, when everyone is still recovering from their weekend and traffic is as light as a feather.

Also, it's crucial to keep in mind the time of year. For example, if you're trying to sell a house in the middle of summer, it's probably not a great idea to have an open house in the middle of a heat wave. Instead, try to schedule it on a day when the weather is as perfect as a spring morning.

It's important to be aware of your own body language and behavior during open houses and other showings. This means smiling, making eye contact, and being welcoming and approachable. Additionally, it's important to be mindful of your own behavior and to avoid smoking, drinking or eating during the showing.

And lastly, make sure your house is in tip-top shape, both inside and out, before any showings. Clean it up like you're getting ready for a royal visit, and make sure everything is in order. Trust me, you don't want potential buyers to see your home and think "this place looks like it's been hit by a hurricane".

Reaching the right buyers

All your marketing efforts don't mean diddly unless you effectively target specific groups of buyers. By understanding the needs and wants of different groups of buyers, you'll be able to tailor your marketing efforts and increase the chances of a successful sale. In this section, we'll take a look at how to target specific groups of buyers, such as first-time home buyers, investors, and retirees.

Learn how to target the right buyers by studying the demographics of your area. Demographics refer to the statistical characteristics of a population, such as age, gender, income, education, and occupation. Marketers often use demographics to segment their target audience and tailor their marketing efforts to specific groups of people. In other words, demographics are like a window into the minds of your target audience. By understanding their age, gender, income, education, and other characteristics, you can get a better idea of what they're looking for in a product or service, and craft your message accordingly. It's like having a crystal ball that allows you to predict what your target audience wants, and tailor your marketing efforts to meet those needs.

First, let's take a look at how to target first-time home buyers. First-time home buyers are typically looking for a home that is affordable, in a good location, and in very good condition. To effectively target first-time home buyers, it's important to highlight the affordability and location of your home in your marketing efforts. This can include things like highlighting the low property taxes, the proximity to schools and public transportation, and any energy-efficient upgrades. "Highlighting these features in your marketing efforts can help attract them," says real estate expert, Barbara Corcoran.

Another group of buyers to consider targeting are investors. Investors are typically looking for a property that has the potential for a good return on investment. To effectively target investors, it's important to highlight any potential rental income or the possibility for future development in the area. Additionally, you can also highlight any renovations or upgrades that have been made to the property, as this can help increase the potential return on investment.

"Investors are looking for properties that have the potential for a good return on investment, highlighting any potential rental income or the possibility for future development in the area can help attract them," says real estate expert Gary Keller.

Lastly, let's take a look at how to target retirees. Retirees are typically looking for a home that is low-maintenance and in a quiet, safe neighborhood. To effectively target retirees, it's important to highlight any low-maintenance features of your home, such as a newly updated roof or easy-care landscaping. Additionally, you can also highlight the safety and quietness of the neighborhood, and the proximity to amenities such as hospitals, shopping, and dining.

By understanding the needs and wants of different groups of buyers, such as first-time home buyers, investors, and retirees, and tailoring your marketing efforts to meet those needs, you'll be able to attract the right buyers for your home. Additionally, it's also important to be flexible and consider other groups of buyers, such as families with children, professionals, and downsizers.

To effectively target different groups of potential buyers, it is crucial to have a deep understanding of their specific needs and wants. This can be achieved by thoroughly researching the demographics of your target audience and identifying what they are looking for in a home.

For example, when I was selling a previous home, I knew that one of my target groups were families with children. Therefore, I made sure to highlight the home's proximity to top-rated schools in the area, as well as the spacious backyard that would be perfect for kids to play in. Additionally, I also emphasized the size of the bedrooms, as well as the amount of storage space that the house had, as these are important factors for families with children.

Another target group I had in mind were professionals who were looking for a home with a dedicated home office, or easy access to transportation. I emphasized the extra room in the house that could be used as an office and the nearby public transportation options, for those who want to have a hybrid work situation, working at home some days, and at an office building on other days.

Lastly, I also targeted downsizers who were looking for a home with low-maintenance features or a smaller yard. I highlighted the fact that the house had a smaller yard that was easy to maintain, as well as the fact that the house had been recently renovated and didn't require much upkeep.

By understanding and highlighting the specific needs and wants of different groups of potential buyers, I was able to effectively target and appeal to them, which ultimately led to a successful sale.

Understanding the demographics of the area where your home is located is crucial. This can include things like the median age, income, and education level of the area. By understanding the demographics of the area, you'll be able to better understand the types of buyers who are most likely to be interested in your home.

One of the first things to consider when researching the demographics of the area is the population. This can include things like the total population of the area, the population density, and the age distribution of the population. This information can be found on websites such as the U.S. Census Bureau and the American Community Survey.

When researching the demographics of an area, it's crucial to consider the income level of the population. This is because the income level can have a significant impact on the housing market and the types of properties that will be in demand. Factors to consider include the median household income, the poverty rate, and the unemployment rate. These statistics can be found on websites such as the U.S. Census Bureau and the American Community Survey.

Understanding the income level of an area can give you a sense of your market and the types of properties people are looking for. It can also reveal the level of affluence and purchasing power of likely buyers, making your marketing more effective.

Another important aspect of researching the demographics of the area is to consider the education level of the population. This includes the percentage of the population with a college degree and the quality of the local schools.

By considering both the income level and education level of the population when researching the demographics of an area, real estate professionals can gain valuable insights into the housing market and target their marketing efforts effectively to potential buyers.

At this point, you might be wondering, "Well, where do I get all this demographic information from?" A lot of it can be found on government websites such as the U.S. Census Bureau and the American Community Survey. And the real estate platforms such as Zillow, Redfin, and Trulia also provide such information and a lot more.

When researching the demographics of the area, it's also important to consider other factors such as the proximity to amenities, the overall feel of the neighborhood, and the local real estate market. As a home seller, you can use this information to tailor your marketing efforts and create a listing that speaks to the demographic of your area.

Listing materials

When it comes to selling your house without a realtor, one of the most important things you can do is to create compelling listing materials that showcase your home in the best light possible. What exactly are listing materials? They're photographs, videos, and descriptions that highlight the best features of your home and make it stand out from the competition. They can be posted online, and they can be printed onto brochures.

As the famous quote by William Shakespeare goes, "All the world's a stage, and all the men and women merely players." In this case, your home is the stage and the listing materials are the players that help to showcase it in the best light possible.

According to a study by the National Association of Realtors, 92 percent of home buyers begin their search online, and high-quality photographs are crucial for making a great first impression.

"A picture is worth a thousand words," as the saying goes, and that's never more true than when it comes to selling your home. When it comes to taking photographs of your home, there are a few things to keep in mind. First, it's important to make sure the photographs are well-lit and show your home in the best possible light. This means avoiding harsh shadows and making sure the rooms are well-lit and free of clutter.

Additionally, it's important to showcase a variety of different rooms and spaces in your home. This will give potential buyers a better idea of what your home has to offer and help them envision themselves living there.

Another important aspect of creating compelling listing materials is showcasing your home in a video. A video can give potential buyers a better sense of the layout and flow of your home, as well as give them a feel for the neighborhood and surrounding area.

When it comes to creating a video of your home, there are a few things to keep in mind. First, it's important to make sure the video is well-lit and free of clutter. Showcase a variety of different rooms and spaces in your home, just like with the photographs.

Finally, it's important to include a detailed and compelling description of your home in your listing materials. This will give potential buyers a better sense of what your home has to offer and help them envision themselves living there.

When it comes to writing a description of your home, there are a few things to keep in mind. First, it's important to focus on the positive aspects of your home and highlight the best features. Additionally, it's important to use descriptive language and paint a vivid picture of your home for potential buyers.

For example, instead of simply saying "the kitchen is updated," you might say "the kitchen boasts sleek stainless steel appliances and granite countertops, making it the perfect space for cooking and entertaining."

Another important aspect of creating compelling listing materials is showcasing the lifestyle that can be enjoyed in your home. This means highlighting the amenities, features and the neighborhood that will make your home an attractive choice for potential buyers. It's important to showcase the sense of community, the proximity to the city, the school district, the parks, the restaurants and any other lifestyle elements that make your home an attractive place to live.

When creating your listing materials, it's important to remember that less is often more. Potential buyers want to see the best features of your home, but they don't want to be overwhelmed with too much information. Keep your photographs, videos and descriptions concise, but also detailed enough to give potential buyers a sense of what your home has to offer.

Another important aspect to keep in mind is to keep your listing materials up-to-date. This means that if you make any changes to your home, such as renovating a room or updating the landscaping, you should update your listing materials to reflect these changes. This will ensure that potential buyers have the most accurate and up-to-date information about your home.

When it comes to selling your home, it's important to remember that first impressions are everything. By creating compelling listing materials that showcase the best features of your home, you'll be able to make a great first impression on potential buyers and increase the chances of your home being sold quickly and for the best price possible.

In the words of the famous real estate author Dale Chumbley, "The key to selling a home is to make it stand out from the crowd. The more unique and appealing your property is, the more likely it is to sell quickly and for top dollar." With this in mind, take the time to showcase your home's unique features and make it stand out from the competition, and you'll be well on your way to a successful sale.

The good, the bad, and the ugly

Can I give an example of an ineffective description of a home for sale, compared to a good one? You bet:

An ineffective description of a house for sale might be something like "3 bedroom, 2 bathroom house for sale. Needs work." Obviously, this description doesn't provide much information and doesn't make the house sound very appealing. It's like a bland dish without any spices, it doesn't entice anyone's taste buds.

On the other hand, an effective description of a house for sale might be something like "Charming 3 bedroom, 2 bathroom cape cod style home for sale. This stunning home features a spacious living room with a cozy fireplace, a beautifully updated kitchen with stainless steel appliances, a formal dining room for hosting dinner parties, and a serene backyard perfect for summer barbecues. The master bedroom suite boasts a walk-in closet and an en suite bathroom. This gem of a home is located in a desirable neighborhood and is just a short walk from parks, shops, and restaurants. Don't miss your chance to make this house your dream home."

This description is like a scrumptious meal with all the right ingredients. It provides detailed information about the house and makes it sound appealing and desirable. It paints a picture of the house, making it easy for potential buyers to envision themselves living there. It also provides a sense of the neighborhood and the lifestyle that the house offers. This type of effective description will make people crave to see the house and make an offer.

.

Zillow, the 10-ton Godzilla, and the rest

Now that we've covered the basics of marketing and its paraphernalia, let's move on to some supercharged tools. In today's digital age, the process of selling a home has become increasingly streamlined. With the help of online platforms such as Zillow, you sell your home more quickly and efficiently than ever before—with or without an agent.

In the real estate world, Zillow is regarded both as a knight in shining armor, and the grim reaper. Many traditional real estate agents see it as their number-one enemy, bent on destroying their market. Other professionals see Zillow as a valuable tool that can bring more business their way.

Zillow is like the Tony Stark of the real estate world, a genius inventor that allows homeowners to list their homes for sale and search for homes to buy, all in one place. With millions of users visiting the site every month, it's no wonder it's one of the most popular platforms for buying and selling homes. The company makes most of its money on advertising—both from home sellers, and from regular real estate agents paying for exposure on the site.

One of the most important ways that Zillow can help you sell your home is through its powerful marketing tools. You can list your home with all the bells and whistles, including photographs, virtual tours and detailed descriptions. And if you want to go the extra mile, Zillow offers sponsored listings to make your home stand out like a beacon in the night. So, whether you see Zillow as a superhero or a super villain, one thing is for sure, it can definitely help you sell your home. Another key advantage of using Zillow is that it makes the process of selling your home more accessible. Unlike traditional real estate agents, Zillow allows you to list your home for sale and handle the negotiations on your own. This means that you are in complete control of the process and can make decisions that are in your best interest. Participating on Zillow allows you to avoid the hassle of creating your own website to advertise your home.

Additionally, Zillow provides you with valuable data about your area and the home selling process. It has a feature that estimates the value of your home, and can also give you an idea of how much similar homes in your area have sold for. It also provides you with information about market trends and housing inventory, which can help you make informed decisions about pricing your home.

One of the most valuable advantages of using Zillow is the ability to connect directly with potential buyers. When a buyer expresses interest in your home on Zillow, you will receive their contact information, allowing you to communicate directly with them. This eliminates the need for a middleman, such as a real estate agent, and allows you to handle all negotiations on your own.

For example, I had a great experience with a potential buyer who was interested in my home listed a couple of years ago on Zillow. I received their contact information, and we were able to communicate directly and arrange a viewing at my convenience. We were able to negotiate the price and closing date without the need of a real estate agent, and closed the sale in a timely manner.

In addition to connecting with buyers, Zillow also allows you to connect with professionals who can help you through the process of selling your home. This includes mortgage lenders, home inspectors, and contractors, to name a few. This allows you to have a one-stop-shop experience, where you can find everything you need to sell your home, all in one place. This made the process of selling my home much more convenient, as I was able to find all the professional I needed just by browsing Zillow.

It's generally free for homeowners to list their home for sale on Zillow. With the FSBO listing, you can include basic information about the property, such as the address, number of bedrooms and bathrooms, square footage, and photos. However, there are a few considerations. First, if your buyer is represented by a traditional real estate agent (which is mostly the case), you'll need to pay that agent the usually one-half of the usual commission, usually 2.5 percent to 3 percent of the sales price.

Zillow also offers paid listing options that allow homeowners to enhance their listing and make it more visible to potential buyers. These "featured listings" enable you to increase visibility and visibility of the listing and also includes the ability to add more photos, videos, and descriptions.

The cost of a featured listing on Zillow can vary depending on the type of listing and the location of the property. Typically, a featured listing on Zillow can cost anywhere from a few hundred dollars to several thousand dollars, depending on the level of exposure and visibility that the listing receives. The cost may also depend on the package you choose, the duration of the listing, and any additional services or features that you may want to add.

Zillow also provides a wide range of free resources and tools to help you navigate the process of selling your home. This includes a seller's guide that provides information on how to prepare your home for sale, how to price your home correctly, and how to handle offers and closing. Additionally, you can access a variety of online guides, videos, and articles that provide information on everything from staging your home to understanding the closing process.

While Zillow is a great resource for homeowners looking to sell their home without an agent, it is important to remember that it is not a substitute for professional advice. It is always a good idea to consult with a lawyer or a real estate attorney to ensure that you are following all the legal requirements and that your sale is in compliance with local laws.

Another great feature of Zillow is its ability to keep track of your home's performance on the market. You will have access to statistics such as how many times your home has been viewed, how many leads you've received, and how many times your home has been shared. You can also track how your home compares to similar homes in your area, which can help you make informed decisions about pricing, marketing, and negotiation.

It's also worth noting that Zillow offers a 3D Home virtual tour feature that can help homeowners showcase their property in a unique and engaging way. This feature allows potential buyers to take a virtual walkthrough of the property, giving them a realistic sense of the layout and flow of the home. This can be especially helpful in attracting buyers who may not be able to physically view the property due to distance, time constraints, or health concerns.

And Zillow provides a platform for homeowners to get feedback from potential buyers, which can help them understand what areas of their home are most appealing or where improvements could be made. This feedback can help homeowners make necessary changes before listing their home, increasing the chances of a successful sale.

Furthermore, Zillow has a feature called "Zillow Open House", where homeowners can schedule open houses and invite potential buyers to view their property. This feature allows homeowners to control the schedule of the open house and to track the attendance of the potential buyers.

This can be a great way to generate interest and leads for your property.

Zillow also has a feature that allows homeowners to track the progress of their sale. This includes information on the status of their listing, how many times it has been viewed, and how many leads have been generated. This feature can help homeowners stay on top of their sale and make any necessary adjustments to their listing or marketing strategy.

Lastly, it's worth noting that Zillow also provides access to a team of experts that can assist homeowners with any questions they may have about the selling process. This team can provide guidance on how to prepare and price your home, how to navigate the legal aspects of selling a home, and how to handle offers and closing.

More choices

At this point, you might be wondering, are there some alternatives to Zillow? Yes, there are several:

- Redfin: A popular online real estate platform that provides a range of services including home listings, home valuations, and home buying and selling resources. (We'll look at Redfin in more detail below.)
- Realtor.com: An online real estate platform owned by the National Association of Realtors that provides access to home listings, home valuations, and home buying and selling resources.

- Trulia: A popular online real estate platform that provides access to home listings, home valuations, and home buying and selling resources. (Trulia is a subsidiary of Zillow, and like Zillow, makes most of its money from advertising).
- Homes.com: An online real estate platform that provides access to home listings, home valuations, and home buying and selling resources.
- Homesnap: A real estate search platform that provides access to home listings, home valuations, and home buying and selling resources.
- Movoto: An online real estate platform that provides access to home listings, home valuations, and home buying and selling resources.
- Realestate.com.au: A leading real estate website in Australia that offers property listings, as well as property research and buying tools.
- Rightmove: A leading real estate website in the UK that offers property listings, as well as property research and buying tools.
- Century 21: A well-known real estate franchise that has an online platform that provides access to home listings, home valuations, and home buying and selling resources.
- Homeseekers.com: A real estate search engine that provides access to home listings, home valuations, and home buying and selling resources.

That's a long list. But there is only one primary competitor to Zillow, and that is Redfin.

Redfin

Redfin is another popular option for homeowners looking to take control of the process. Redfin is an online real estate platform that provides a range of services, including home listings, home valuations, and home buying and selling resources. In this chapter, we will explore how FSBOs can use Redfin to sell their home, the advantages and disadvantages of using the platform, and how it compares to Zillow.

One way to compare Redfin and Zillow is the amount of traffic to their respective websites. The number of visitors to Zillow and Redfin's websites shows that Zillow has a ton more traffic. According to data from SimilarWeb, Zillow's website has an average of around 200 million monthly visitors, while Redfin has an average of around 30 million monthly visitors. Zillow is also considered to be the most popular real estate website in the country, with a market share of around 50 pecent of all real estate website traffic, while Redfin's market share is around 3 percent. So, Redfin's smaller share of home shoppers makes it harder for FSBOs to generate leads and attract potential buyers compared to Zillow. But it doesn't hurt to try them. Like the Avis car-rental company, number two usually tries harder.

However, one of the key features that sets Redfin apart from the rest is that Redfin has its own team of agents and brokerages that can provide additional support and assistance to homeowners. By contrast, Zillow outsources their agent jobs.

Unlike traditional agents who are motivated mostly by commissions, many Redfin agents are independent contractors paid on a per-job basis. For example, these folks might be paid $50 or $75 dollars to show a house to a prospective buyer, depending on how expensive the market is in their area. These agents are working less like a traditional agent, and more like a glorified Uber driver—they drive to the house, meet the home shopper and open the door. So Redfin agents generally have much less experience and connections than traditional real estate agents.

However, not all of Redfin's agents are simply door-openers, and those higher up on the food chain are called "Redfin Agents". They are licensed real estate agents who are trained to provide guidance and support to homeowners throughout the home selling process. They can help FSBOs with pricing, marketing, and negotiations, as well as provide advice on local market conditions. Buyers and sellers pay 1 percent commission, a nice discount compared to traditional agents.

Redfin Agents are incentivized to sell the home for the best price possible, as their commission is based on the sale price.

It's worth noting that Redfin is currently only available in certain markets within the United States, so it may not be an option for all FSBOs.

Redfin Agents can provide FSBOs with exposure to a wider pool of buyers and sellers than they would have on their own and can also provide access to additional online resources and tools, such as a home value estimator and a home improvement cost estimator, which can help homeowners price their home correctly and make informed decisions about the sale. Additionally, Redfin Agents can also provide additional support during the closing process, which can be a critical stage of the sale.

In conclusion, Redfin Agents can provide a valuable service to homeowners who are selling their home without the assistance of a real estate agent. They can provide professional advice and guidance throughout the home selling process, including pricing, marketing, and negotiation. Additionally, they can provide access to a wider pool of buyers and sellers, as well as additional online resources and tools. Additionally, Redfin Agents will also assist with the closing process and if the homeowner is looking to buy another property, Redfin Agent can help with that too. It's important to note that while Redfin Agents can provide valuable support, FSBOs should still consult with a lawyer or real estate attorney to ensure compliance with local laws.

Another option: flat-fee listing services

For home sellers who want to save some money, retain control over the selling process, but also want assistance with the nitty-gritty details of home selling, flat-fee listing services are an enticing option. These services offer a unique advantage, providing access to the coveted local Multiple Listing Service (MLS), a treasure trove of real estate listings and information. This powerful tool, utilized by agents and brokers alike, serves as a central hub where properties can be listed, information can be shared, and access to other agents and brokers can be gained. The MLS enables agents and brokers to seamlessly work together, streamlining the process and ultimately increasing the chances of a successful sale.

The MLS typically includes information such as the property's address, price, number of bedrooms and bathrooms, square footage, and photographs. It also includes information about the property's location, such as the neighborhood, school district, and nearby amenities. The MLS also includes information about the property's history, such as how long it has been on the market and any recent price changes.

By the way, the big search sites like Zillow are not an MLS, even though they're often mistaken as one—there's a lot of properties they don't list, like FSBOs from other companies, auctions and foreclosures. Most real estate agents believe that an MLS is a more effective way to sell or buy properties. Instead, Zillow is a real estate database and marketing company, offering advertising opportunities. In other words, it's a powerful tool, but it should be used in conjunction with other resources to achieve optimal results.

Every flat-fee company is different and charges different fees. Here are some examples of the differences, which can affect the price by a wide margin:

1. Listing fee: This is a one-time fee that is charged to list the property on the Multiple Listing Service (MLS) and other online platforms. This fee can vary depending on the company and the region, but it can range from a few hundred to a few thousand dollars.

2. Marketing and advertising fees: Some flat-fee listing services may charge additional fees for marketing and advertising services, such as professional photography, staging, or online advertising.

3. Extra services fees: Some flat-fee listing services may charge extra for additional services such as open house coordination, showing coordination, negotiations, paperwork and closing coordination.

4. Commission fee: Some flat-fee listing services may charge a commission fee if the property is sold by another agent, who is not part of the flat-fee service provider. This can vary from company

to company, but it is typically a percentage of the sale price.

"Using a flat-fee broker to sell my home was a great experience," said Lester. "I was able to save thousands of dollars on commission fees, while still getting top-notch service and support from the broker's team.

"I was really impressed with how easy the process was with the flat-fee broker. They provided me with all the necessary tools and resources to list my property, and their website made it simple for me to manage my listing and track the progress of the sale.

"The broker's team was very responsive and answered all of my questions in a timely manner. They were also very helpful in providing me with tips and advice on how to market my property and attract potential buyers.

"I was really impressed with the professional photography and staging services that were provided. It made my property look amazing online and in person, which helped to attract more buyers.

They also provided me with access to their network of local agents, which helped to increase the exposure of my property. This resulted in multiple offers, and I was able to close the sale quickly and at the price I wanted.

"I was really pleased with the outcome. I sold my property for a great price and saved a lot of money on commission fees. I highly recommend using a flat-fee broker to anyone looking to sell their home."

The MLS is a powerful tool for real estate agents and brokers because it allows them to quickly and easily access a wide range of information about properties that are for sale. This information can be used to help agents and brokers match buyers with properties that meet their needs, and to help sellers market their properties more effectively. Additionally, the MLS allows agents and brokers to collaborate and share information, which can lead to more sales and higher commissions.

Here are your choices:

- Redfin: We've mentioned them before. One of their offerings is a flat-fee service for home sellers. They charge a listing fee of 1.5 percent to list a home and handle the sale, which is significantly less than the traditional commission of 2 percent to 3 percent.
- When it comes to flat-fee home selling services in the United States, there are a few that stand out as the most well-known and reputable options.

- First on the list is Redfin, the Seattle-based real estate brokerage that has made waves in the industry with their innovative flat-fee model. For just 1.5% of the final sale price, Redfin will list your home and handle the sale from start to finish, saving you thousands of dollars in commission fees compared to the traditional 2-3% charged by most real estate agents. They have a reputation for providing excellent customer service.
- Next up, we have Purplebricks, the UK-based real estate agency that has recently expanded to the USA. With their flat-fee model, Purplebricks charges a fixed fee of $3,200 to list your property and handle the sale, regardless of the final sale price. This means you can save big on commission fees, while still getting access to their top-notch agents and cutting-edge technology.
- Another great option is Clever Real Estate, a flat-fee service that connects home sellers with local real estate agents who offer discounted commission rates. For just $3,000, Clever will list your home and handle the sale, giving you access to top-notch agents at a fraction of the cost. Also, Clever's partnerships with top-notch brokerages such as Berkshire Hathaway and RE/MAX allow them to offer a unique advantage to their clients. By teaming up with these industry giants, Clever promises to deliver the expertise and guidance of a full-service agent, all while keeping costs minimal. So, if you're looking to sell your home with the support

of a professional and save money, Clever may be the perfect fit for you.

- And last but not least, we have Homie and EasyKnock, both of which offer flat-fee services for home sellers. Homie charges a flat fee of $3,500 to list your home and handle the sale, while EasyKnock charges $3,995 for the same services.

All of these flat-fee home selling services offer an excellent value proposition for homeowners looking to save money on commission fees while still getting top-notch service and support. Whether you're looking to save thousands of dollars, have access to cutting-edge technology, or work with experienced local agents, these companies are definitely worth checking out.

And let's not forget about the added benefits of using a flat-fee service like these. For starters, you have more control over the sale of your home. You can set your own price, choose your own closing date, and make all the decisions about how your home is marketed and sold.

Additionally, with a flat-fee service, you have access to the same resources and technology as traditional real estate agents, such as professional photography and staging services, online marketing, and more. This means your home will be presented in the best possible light to potential buyers, increasing the chances of a quick and profitable sale.

Another great aspect of flat-fee services is that you can save money without compromising on service. The agents and staff at these companies are just as dedicated to helping you sell your home as traditional agents, but at a much lower cost.

It's also worth noting that flat-fee home selling services can be a great option for homeowners who are comfortable with the selling process and want to be more hands-on. These services typically provide a more streamlined, do-it-yourself approach to selling, allowing you to handle many of the details yourself, such as scheduling showings and negotiating with buyers.

However, it's important to keep in mind that while flat-fee services can save you money, they may not be the best option for everyone. For example, if you're not comfortable with the selling process or don't have the time to handle the details yourself, a traditional full-service agent may be a better choice. Additionally, if your home is located in a high-end luxury market, it may be more beneficial to work with a traditional agent who specializes in that market and has the resources and contacts to sell your home for top dollar.

And not everyone has a good experience going this route:

I was really excited to use a flat-fee broker to save money on commission fees, but my experience was really disappointing, said Kelly. "The broker's team was not very responsive and it took them a long time to answer my questions or provide me with the information I needed.

"The marketing and advertising of my property was not as professional as I expected. The photos were not good quality and the online listing was not well done, which made it difficult to attract potential buyers. I felt like I was on my own throughout the process and did not receive the support and guidance I needed to sell my property.

"In the end, my property took much longer to sell than I expected and I didn't end up saving as much money as I thought I would with the flat-fee broker. I wouldn't recommend this type of service to anyone. I believe that for the money I paid, I deserved better service and support."

So, your mileage may vary regarding flat-fee service. It's worth mentioning that some local brokers offer such services, and it would be easier for you to find online reviews of these businesses. With the big national companies, their service quality can vary according to the conditions in different communities. '

Some regions may have more competition and more demanding customers, which can affect the quality of service provided. And, like any business, even the best brokers may have some bad reviews or unhappy customers. Consumers who feel they've gotten a raw deal are the most likely to write reviews (and scathing ones!) more likely than those who were satisfied. It's always good to check multiple sources such as online reviews, recommendations from friends or family, and compare services and fees offered by different companies before making a decision.

Wheeling and dealing

When it comes to selling real estate, negotiating is where the magic happens. It's the moment when buyers and sellers come together to haggle, bargain, and make a deal. Think of it like a game of poker, but instead of cards, you're playing with square footage and curb appeal. The key to a successful negotiation is to come prepared with all the facts, figures, and counter offers at your fingertips. It's not just about getting the highest price, it's about finding a mutually beneficial agreement that satisfies both parties. Remember, in real estate, "everything is negotiable," so don't be afraid to ask for what you want and be willing to compromise. And always keep in mind, the best deal is the one where both parties walk away feeling like they won.

Here are a few examples:

- Price: The most obvious and important thing to negotiate is the price of the property. Both the buyer and seller will want to get the best deal possible.
- Closing costs: Closing costs are the expenses associated with the purchase of a property, such as title insurance, appraisal fees, and attorney's fees. These costs can be negotiated between the buyer and seller.
- Closing date: The closing date is the date when the sale of the property is completed and the buyer takes possession of the property. The closing date can be

negotiated between the buyer and seller, depending on their schedules and the availability of the property.

- Repairs and inspections: Any repairs or inspections that need to be made to the property before the sale can be negotiated between the buyer and seller. The buyer may request that certain repairs be made before the sale, or that certain inspections be done, and the seller may agree to make certain repairs or pay for certain inspections.
- Financing: The terms of the financing can also be negotiated. For example, the buyer may ask for a lower interest rate or a longer amortization period.
- Contingencies: Contingencies are conditions that must be met before the sale can be completed. For example, the sale of the property may be contingent on the buyer selling their current home.
- Inclusions and exclusions: what will be included in the sale, such as appliances, and what will be excluded, such as personal items, can be negotiated
- Rent-back: some sellers might want to stay in the property for a short period after closing, this can also be negotiated and agreed upon by both parties.

These are just a few examples of the most common things that can be negotiated in a real estate transaction. The specific terms of the sale will depend on the needs and preferences of the buyer and seller, as well as the specific conditions of the market.

Let's take a look at how to navigate the negotiation process and close the sale successfully. We'll also provide examples of the author's own experience and some tips and advice from real estate experts.

The first step in negotiating and closing a sale is to understand the market conditions. This means knowing the average price of similar homes in the area, as well as any market trends that may be affecting the sale of your home.

Home sellers can determine the average price of similar homes that have sold in their community by researching comparable sales in the area. There are several ways to do this:

- Look at public records: Public records, such as property tax records, can provide information on the sale price of homes in the area. You can find this information on the website of your local county or municipal government.
- Use online real estate databases: Websites such as Zillow, Redfin, and Realtor.com, provide information on recent home sales in a specific area. You can search for homes by location, type, and price range, and get a general idea of the average price of similar homes that have sold in your community.
- Consult with a real estate agent: A real estate agent can provide you with a Comparative Market Analysis (CMA) which is a report that compares your home to similar homes that have sold in the area. This report

will give you a detailed analysis of the prices of similar homes, including the average price. Will a real estate agent do this for free, even though you're not a client? The smart agents certainly will, because they know that demonstrating their competence to you gets their foot in the door to gain you as a client in the future, or that you'll send them referrals—friends and family who need an agent. If an agent won't do a CMA for you, they're either lazy or ignorant—or both.

Additionally, it's important to have a good understanding of your own needs and priorities, such as how quickly you need to sell your home and whether you're willing to make any concessions.

The appraisal

We've touched on the topic of appraisals a few times already, now let's take a deeper dive.

Ultimately, the process that determines your home's value is the appraisal. A real estate appraisal is a professional assessment of the value of a piece of property. It is typically done to determine the fair market value of a home or other piece of real estate. This can be used for a variety of purposes, such as determining the value for a sale or refinance, assessing property taxes, or determining the value for insurance purposes.

Typically, the party ordering the appraisal, such as the buyer or the lender, pays for the real estate appraisal.

However, the specific details of who pays for the appraisal may vary depending on the situation and the terms of the agreement between the parties involved.

The appraisal is typically done by a professional appraiser, who is a licensed and trained expert in evaluating real estate. The appraiser will typically conduct a thorough examination of the property, including measurements of the structure and land, as well as an assessment of any improvements or upgrades that have been made. They will also take into account factors such as location, comparable sales in the area, and current market conditions.

The possible results of a real estate appraisal can vary, depending on the specific property and market conditions. The appraised value may be higher or lower than the asking price or the price that a buyer is willing to pay. If the appraised value is lower than the purchase price, the lender may require the buyer to pay the difference in cash or to renegotiate the purchase price. If the appraised value is higher than the purchase price, the lender may be willing to loan more money, giving the buyer more flexibility in the purchase.

As we hinted earlier, appraisals are usually commissioned by buyers or the buyer's lender, but a lot of folks are interested in the appraisal:

- Buyers and Sellers: A buyer or seller may request an appraisal to help determine a fair purchase or sales price for a property.

- Government agencies: Appraisals may be required for property tax assessments or eminent domain proceedings.
- Insurance companies: Appraisals may be required for insurance purposes, such as determining the replacement cost of a property for insurance coverage.
- Investors: Appraisals can be useful for investors as well, to determine the value of a property they may consider buying, holding, or renovating as a rental property or flipping.

The contract

Once you've reached an agreement with the potential buyer, the next step is to draw up the purchase contract. This is like signing a marriage certificate but instead of a lifetime commitment, it's just a commitment to a piece of land. This legally binding document outlines all the nitty-gritty details of the sale, including the purchase price, closing date, and any contingencies. Think of it like the blueprint for the building of your financial future.

It's also important to be aware of the closing process and to have all necessary documents in order, such as the title, property survey, and any disclosures. Additionally, it's a good idea to hire a closing agent who can handle the transfer of funds and the recording of the deed.

Mark, a home seller, was preparing to sell his house. He had lived in the house for many years and had made many updates and improvements to it over time. He was excited to move on to the next chapter of his life, but he knew that the process of selling a house could be complicated and time-consuming.

One day, while chatting with a friend, the friend recommended Jane, a closing agent. A closing agent is a professional who specializes in handling all of the legal and administrative aspects of the home-selling process.

Mark decided to contact Jane, the closing agent, and set up a meeting. During the meeting, Jane explained the services she could offer and the benefits of having a closing agent. "I can help you with everything from reviewing and preparing all of the necessary paperwork, handling the closing process, and ensuring that all deadlines are met," Jane said. "My goal is to make the process as smooth as possible for you. But let me tell you, it's not an easy job, there are a lot of legal requirements, and deadlines that need to be met, and if something is missed, it could delay the whole process or even fall through."

Mark was impressed with Jane's experience and professionalism, and he decided to hire her as his closing agent.

Throughout the process, Jane provided Mark with valuable advice and insights, and she was always available to answer any questions he had. She made sure all the deadlines were met, including the title search, home inspection, and the appraisal. She also arranged for all the necessary documentation, such as the purchase agreement and the closing documents. She was constantly communicating with all the parties involved, keeping track of the progress, and making sure everything was in order.

Thanks to Jane's help, the process went smoothly, and Mark was able to sell his house at the price he was looking for. Mark was very grateful for the headaches that Jane prevented him from going through, and he felt relieved that he didn't have to handle all the legal and administrative aspects of the process on his own.

Good communication is a must. This means keeping open lines of communication with the potential buyer and being responsive to their questions and concerns. Additionally, it's important to keep your real estate attorney and closing agent informed of any changes or developments in the sale.

It's also important to be aware of the deadlines and contingencies in the purchase contract and to make sure that they are met in a timely manner. This includes things like completing inspections, obtaining financing, and transferring the title.

Another important aspect of negotiating and closing a sale is understanding the tax implications. This means being aware of any capital gains tax or other taxes that may be due as a result of the sale. Additionally, it's important to consult with a tax professional to ensure that you are aware of any tax implications and that you are taking the necessary steps to minimize them.

Another important aspect to keep in mind when negotiating and closing a sale is to be aware of the legal and regulatory requirements. This means understanding the legal documents involved in the sale, such as the purchase contract and the deed, as well as any state and federal laws that may apply. It's important to have a good understanding of these requirements and to seek the advice of a real estate attorney if necessary.

When negotiating and closing the sale, it's also important to be aware of the potential risks involved and to take steps to minimize them. This includes things like making sure that the property is properly inspected and that any repairs are made, as well as ensuring that the buyer is financially capable of completing the purchase.

Closing the door

When closing the sale, it's also important to be aware of the timing and to make sure that everything is done in a timely manner. This includes things like getting the property inspected, obtaining financing, and transferring the title. It's important to be aware of the deadlines and to make sure that everything is done on time to avoid delays and complications.

Another important aspect to keep in mind when negotiating and closing a sale is to be aware of the home's condition and to make any necessary repairs or improvements. This includes things like painting, cleaning, and making any necessary repairs. Additionally, it's important to disclose any known issues or defects with the property.

Negotiating for the highest price

Being prepared is key for effective negotiation. Here are some tips:

- Have a solid understanding of your home's value and being able to justify any asking price. Additionally, it's important to be flexible and willing to make concessions, such as offering closing cost assistance or making repairs to the home.
- Be aware of the home's unique selling points and to highlight them to potential buyers. This includes things like location, size, and amenities. Additionally, it's important to make sure that your home is in the best possible condition, as this can increase its perceived value.

- Be flexible: Be open to negotiation and consider different offers. You never know what a buyer might be willing to pay or what concessions they may be willing to make.
- Highlight the unique features of your property: Point out the special features of your property and how they add value. For example, if you have a recently renovated kitchen, be sure to mention it.
- Be confident: Show the buyer that you believe in your property and that you're confident in its value. This will help them see the value too.

Be prepared to walk away: If the buyer's offer is too low, don't be afraid to walk away. This can show that you're serious about getting top dollar and that you're not willing to settle for less.

Let's consider an example of a successful negotiation in a real estate transaction:

Let's say you're the seller of a property that's listed at $500,000. A buyer expresses interest and tours the property, but they come back to you with an offer of $475,000. You might be tempted to reject the offer outright, but remember, negotiation is a two-way street.

Instead of shutting down the offer, try to understand the buyer's perspective. Ask questions and listen to their reasons for thinking the property is worth $475,000. They may have noticed something that you hadn't considered.

Once you've heard them out, it's your turn to share why you think the property is worth more. Highlight the unique features and recent upgrades that add value to your property. Be confident in your asking price, but also be open to compromise.

With a bit of back and forth, you might find that the buyer is willing to meet you at a price point of $485,000, which is $5,000 more than their original offer but still less than your original asking price, but still a win-win situation.

Sarah had lived in her house for over a decade. She had raised her children there and had made many updates and improvements to the property over the years, including a new roof, updated kitchen, and remodeled bathrooms. She also made sure that the house was clean and well-maintained, with a neutral color palette throughout, to make it more appealing to potential buyers. When the time came to sell the house, Sarah knew that it was in great condition and that it was worth more than most comparable houses in the area.

One day, Michael came to view the house. He was immediately impressed by the condition and layout of the house, and the location was ideal for him. He made an offer, but it was significantly lower than the asking price.

Sarah knew that the house was worth more than the offer, so she decided to negotiate with Michael.

Sarah began by highlighting all of the updates and improvements she had made to the house, including the new roof, updated kitchen, and remodeled bathrooms. She also emphasized the desirable location of the house, close to good schools and shopping centers, and shared some of the future plans for the neighborhood, that she knew from her research.

Michael was impressed by the updates and agreed to raise his offer, but it was still lower than Sarah's asking price. Sarah knew she had to stand firm and not accept less than what she believed the house was worth. She prepared a detailed comparison report of similar houses that were sold in the area, with the prices, features, and the time they were on the market, to back her asking price.

Finally, after several rounds of negotiation, Michael agreed to pay the full asking price for the house. Sarah was thrilled and felt confident that she had gotten the best price for her beloved home, and she felt satisfied that she had done everything she could to showcase the value of her property.

In the end, remember that the goal is to reach a mutually beneficial agreement, so be open, listen and have a positive attitude throughout the process and you'll be able to successfully negotiate and get top dollar for your property. Patience pays off.

In conclusion, negotiating and closing a sale can be a complex process, but by understanding the market conditions, being prepared, being flexible, having an attorney review the purchase contract, being aware of the closing process, hiring a closing agent, keeping open lines of communication, meeting deadlines and contingencies, understanding the tax implications, being aware of the legal and regulatory requirements, being aware of the closing costs and minimizing the risks involved, being mindful of the contingencies and timing, and being aware of the home's condition, you'll be able to successfully navigate the process and close the sale. With these tips in mind, you'll be well on your way to a successful sale and a successful home-selling experience without a realtor.

John and his wife had lived in their home for over 20 years and had raised their children there. They had a lot of sentimental attachment to the home and had made many renovations and improvements over the years. They had decided to downsize and move to a smaller home but they wanted to sell their current house on their own, without the help of a real estate agent.

They did their research and looked at other homes in the area that were similar to theirs. They believed that their house was in a better condition and had more amenities than the others, so they decided to price it higher. They listed it at $700,000, which they thought was fair given the condition and location of their home.

However, their house didn't generate much interest. The few buyers who came to see it were put off by the high price and the fact that it was not in move-in condition. John and his wife were stubborn and refused to lower the price, believing that the house was worth what they were asking for. They even turned down an offer for $650,000, thinking they could get more.

Months passed and their house remained unsold. They became increasingly frustrated as they saw similar houses in the area sell quickly for lower prices. They were emotionally attached to the house and did not want to let it go for a price that they thought was too low.

Eventually, they realized that they had priced the house too high and that they needed to lower the price to be competitive in the market. They hired a real estate agent who helped them price the house correctly and stage it in a way that would appeal to buyers. They finally sold the house for $625,000, which was still a good price, but they had lost thousands of dollars by not pricing it correctly and being stubborn in the beginning. They learned that sometimes it's better to trust the professionals and let them *handle the process of selling a home, as they have the knowledge, experience, and expertise to price a home correctly and market it effectively. They also learned that being emotionally attached to a home can cloud their judgment when it comes to pricing and negotiating with buyers. They also missed the opportunity to sell the house quickly and at a better price due to their lack of marketing skills and experience.*

After the sale, John and his wife realized that hiring an agent would have saved them a lot of stress and money. They also realized that they could have saved a lot of time and hassle if they had hired an agent from the start. They learned that selling a home is not just about pricing it correctly, but also about marketing it effectively and negotiating with buyers. They understood that a good real estate agent can help you price your home correctly, stage it effectively, and market it to the right audience, which can ultimately lead to a faster and more profitable sale.

Contingencies

Contingencies and contingencies agreements are part of the process. Contingencies are conditions or clauses that must be met before the sale can be completed. They are included in the purchase contract and serve as a way to protect both the buyer and the seller.

For the buyer, contingencies provide an opportunity to back out of the transaction if certain conditions are not met. For example, if the buyer includes a financing contingency in the purchase contract, and they are not able to obtain financing, they can back out of the sale without any penalties. Similarly, if the property does not pass the inspection or the appraisal is lower than the agreed upon purchase price, the buyer can also back out of the transaction.

For the seller, contingencies serve as a way to ensure that the buyer is serious about purchasing the property and that they have the means to do so. They also protect the seller from any unexpected surprises that could arise during the sale process.

Overall, contingencies are a way for both buyers and sellers to protect their interests and minimize the risk involved in a real estate transaction.

Here are the most common contingencies in a real estate transaction:

Financing: The sale of the property is contingent on the buyer obtaining financing from a lender.

Home inspection: The sale of the property is contingent on the outcome of a home inspection. If the inspection reveals any issues that the buyer is not comfortable with, they can back out of the sale.

Appraisal: The sale of the property is contingent on the property appraising for at least the purchase price.

Title: The sale of the property is contingent on the title being clear and free of any liens or encumbrances.

Sale of current home: The sale of the property is contingent on the buyer selling their current home.

Homeowners association (HOA) approval: The sale of the property is contingent on the buyer being approved by the homeowners association (HOA), and the buyer agreeing to abide by the HOA rules.

Zoning and permits: The sale of the property is contingent on the property being in compliance with local zoning laws and having all necessary permits.

Lead-based paint: The sale of the property is contingent on the property passing lead-based paint inspections

Flood zone: The sale of the property is contingent on the property not being in a flood zone.

Radon test: The sale of the property is contingent on the property passing a radon test.

These are some of the most common contingencies that can be included in a real estate transaction, but the specific contingencies will depend on the needs and preferences of the buyer and seller, as well as local laws and regulations.

Hiring a lawyer

You might wonder: Do I really need a real estate attorney? I've never even heard of real estate lawyers!

It can be smart to hire a real estate attorney when you are selling or buying a property, particularly if there are any legal complexities or issues involved.

In the world of real estate, it never hurts to seek out an expert opinion. "Having a lawyer review the purchase contract can ensure that your rights are protected and that the contract is fair," says real estate expert Gary Keller.

Here are a few examples of situations where it may be beneficial to hire a real estate attorney:

- If you are selling or buying a property with a complicated title or ownership history. An attorney can help you navigate any legal issues and ensure that the title is transferred correctly.
- If you are selling or buying a property that has liens or other legal encumbrances. An attorney can help you understand and resolve these issues before closing the sale.
- If you are buying or selling a property that is part of a probate or estate sale. An attorney can help you

understand and navigate the legal requirements and procedures involved.

- If you are selling or buying a property that has zoning or land use issues. An attorney can help you understand and comply with any local regulations or restrictions.

- If you are involved in a dispute with the buyer or seller. An attorney can help you navigate and resolve any disputes that may arise during the sale process.

Nobody is going to force you to hire a lawyer, but it's still a good idea to consult with an attorney to review your contract, the title and any other legal documents related to the sale. It's important to note that a real estate attorney can provide a valuable service by reviewing the legal documents, and ensure that everything is done correctly and legally, avoiding future problems.

An attorney can help you navigate local government requirements regarding FSBO transactions. The types of guidelines given by states regarding FSBOs can vary, but some common types include:

- Disclosure requirements: Many states require FSBO sellers to provide certain disclosures to potential buyers, such as information about known defects in the property and any natural hazards in the area.

- Property condition disclosure: Some states require FSBO sellers to provide a property condition disclosure statement to potential buyers, which includes information about any known defects in the property.

- Handling of earnest (deposit) money: FSBO sellers are often required to comply with state laws regarding the handling of earnest money, which is a deposit made by the buyer to show their commitment to the purchase.
- Execution of the sales contract: FSBO sellers are often required to comply with state laws regarding the execution of the sales contract, including the requirement to use a specific form or to have the contract reviewed by an attorney.
- Advertising and marketing: Some states have regulations on how FSBOs can advertise and market their property, such as not being able to imply that they are a licensed agent.
- Tax laws: FSBOs are responsible for adhering to state and local tax laws when selling a property.
- It's important to note that each state has its own specific laws and regulations regarding FSBOs, and it is essential for individuals to check with their state's real estate commission or consult with an attorney to understand the specific guidelines that apply to them.
- Licensing requirement: Some states require FSBOs to have a real estate license if they are receiving a commission or compensation for the sale of a property.
- Mediation: Some states require FSBOs to participate in mediation in case of disputes with buyers.

- Closing and Escrow: FSBOs are often required to comply with state laws regarding closing and escrow, including the use of a title company or attorney to handle the transfer of ownership.
- Fair housing laws: FSBOs are required to comply with fair housing laws and regulations and to not discriminate based on race, color, religion, sex, national origin, disability, and familial status.

It's important to note that the laws and regulations regarding FSBOs can be complex and can vary by state. It is essential for individuals to check with their state's real estate commission or consult with an attorney to understand the specific guidelines that apply to them.

Final pearls of wisdom

"The three most important things in real estate are location, location, location." - Harold Samuel coined this phrase in 1944 when he founded Land Securities.

"The best investment on earth is earth." - This quote is often attributed to Louis Glickman, highlighting the potential for real estate as an investment when selling.

"The best time to sell a home is when the market is hot." - This quote is often attributed to various real estate professionals, emphasizing the importance of timing.

"Price it right and it will sell overnight, price it wrong and it will sit forever." - This quote is often attributed to various real estate professionals.

"A good real estate [seller] is not a salesperson, they're a marketer." - Zig Ziglar, emphasizing the importance of marketing when selling a home.

"The only thing worse than being overpriced is being forgotten." - This quote is often attributed to various real estate professionals, emphasizing the importance of being competitive in the market when selling a home.

"In real estate, the only thing that matters is the last thing that happened." - This quote is often attributed to various real estate professionals, emphasizing the importance of staying current and adapting to market changes when selling a home.

"You make your money when you buy, not when you sell."
- Warren Buffett, emphasizing the importance of making
smart purchasing decisions when investing in real estate to
maximize profits when selling.

"It's not about the listing, it's about the lifestyle." -
Barbara Corcoran, emphasizing the importance of
showcasing the lifestyle benefits of a property when selling.

"A good real estate [seller] is like a good doctor, they
diagnose the problem and prescribe the cure." - This quote is
often attributed to Robert R. Ringer, emphasizing the
importance of understanding the market and identifying
solutions when selling a home.

"It's not about the price, it's about the value." - Tim
Leffel, emphasizing the importance of showcasing the value
of a property when selling.

"Real estate is not about things, it's about relationships."
- Tim and Julie Harris, emphasizing the importance of
building relationships and networking when selling a home.

"In real estate, the difference between good and great is
just a few degrees." - David Meerman Scott, emphasizing the
importance of small changes that can make a big difference
when selling a home.

"The best way to sell a house is to make it irresistible." -
Brian Buffini, emphasizing the importance of making the
property attractive and desirable to potential buyers when
selling.

"The best way to sell a home is to sell the dream, not the house." - Tom Hopkins, emphasizing the importance of marketing the lifestyle benefits of a property when selling.

"The real estate industry is a people business, not a property business." - Todd Duncan, emphasizing the importance of building relationships and networking when selling a home.

"In real estate, the only constant is change." - This quote is often attributed to various real estate professionals, emphasizing the dynamic nature of the real estate market and the need to adapt accordingly when selling.

"Real estate cannot be lost or stolen, nor can it be carried away. Purchased with common sense, paid for in full, and managed with reasonable care, it is about the safest investment in the world." - Franklin D. Roosevelt, emphasizing the stability and safety of investing in real estate.

"A house is made of bricks and beams. A home is made of hopes and dreams." - William C. Payne, emphasizing the emotional aspect of selling a home.

"The best way to predict the future of real estate is to create it." - Abraham Lincoln, emphasizing the importance of innovation and forward-thinking in the real estate industry.

"Buyers decide in the first eight seconds of seeing a home if they're interested in buying it. Get out of your car, walk in their shoes and see what they see within the first eight seconds." – Barbara Corcoran

"The best thing about flipping houses is that it's a lot like playing Monopoly. You buy properties, collect rent, and watch your empire grow." - Scott McGillivray, emphasizing the potential for profits through flipping properties.

"Not following up with your prospects is the same as filling up your bathtub without first putting the stopper in the drain." – Michelle Moore

"The best real estate investments are the ones you don't make." - Donald Trump, emphasizing the importance of careful consideration and avoiding bad investments in the real estate market.

"Buy land, they're not making it anymore." – Mark Twain

Made in the USA
Middletown, DE
08 October 2023

40449452R00070